LATIN AMERICAN BIBLIOGRAPHY

LATIN AMERICAN BIBLIOGRAPHY

A GUIDE

To sources of Information & Research

By

JULIA GARLANT, MA
  British Library of Political & Economic Science

LAURENCE HALLEWELL, PhD, FLA
  School of Oriental & African Studies

BRIGID M. HARRINGTON, BA, DipLib, ALA
  Institute of Latin American Studies, London

MARIA LANDAU, BSc
  Science Reference Library

ELIZABETH LONG, B Phil, MA
  formerly, Institute of Latin American Studies, London

BERNARD NAYLOR, MA, DipLib, ALA
  University of Southampton

PATRICIA NOBLE, BA
  University of London Library

ROBIN M. PRICE, MA, ALA
  Wellcome Historical Medical Library

MICHAEL H. ROGERS, MA, ALA
  Institute of Development Studies, University of Sussex

COLIN R. STEELE, MA, DipLib, ALA
  Australian National University

SARAH TYACKE, BA
  Map Library, British Library

Edited by

LAURENCE HALLEWELL

With a Foreword by

Professor JOHN LYNCH
  Director of the Institute of Latin American
  Studies of the University of London

Published for the SCONUL Latin American Group by the

Institute of Latin American Studies

and distributed from the Library of the School of Oriental
and African Studies

London, 1978

British Library Cataloguing in publication data

Latin American bibliography.
    1. Latin American studies   2. Latin
    America - Bibliography   3. Latin
    America - Information services
    I. Hallewell, Laurence   II. University
    of London, Institute of Latin American
    Studies   III. Standing Conference of National
    and University Libraries, Latin American
    Group
    980'.07   Z1601

ISBN 0-901145-26-2

© SCONUL 1978

Printed at the School of Oriental and African Studies,
University of London

FOREWORD

The sources of Latin American studies are diverse and constantly expanding. In recent years information techniques and services have multiplied so rapidly that the individual researcher often does not know the range of material available. Specialist bibliographies there are in abundance, and also guides to particular collections. But students and teachers have long felt the need of a basic introduction to sources of information and research. We hope the present Guide will meet their needs. Whether they are compiling a bibliography, assembling archival sources, searching for a thesis, or locating computerised data, students now have a permanent aid to research, the equivalent of a seminar course in bibliography, with the added advantage that each of its many sections is compiled by a specialist and takes particular account of sources available in the United Kingdom.

The Latin American Group of the Standing Conference of National and University Libraries (SCONUL) was established in 1972 and continually explores ways in which Latin American materials can be expanded and exploited. From its initiative the present Guide has emerged, the work of eleven librarians experienced in the field of Latin American and Caribbean studies. Researchers will soon appreciate that they are indebted to the practical sense as well as to the special knowledge of Dr. Hallewell and his colleagues. The Institute of Latin American Studies, which houses the Union Catalogue of Latin American Library Materials, is happy to publish the result of their endeavours and to bring it within reach of students, researchers, teachers and all those engaged in Latin American studies.

J. Lynch
Institute of Latin American Studies

CONTENTS

Contents

Contents

Contents

A NOTE ON COVERAGE

Latin America

The expression 'Latin America' dates from the end of last
century, and seems to have been of French coinage, to denote
the Romance (i.e. Spanish, Portuguese and French) speaking
regions of the New World. Of late, particularly in North
American usage, it has been extended to the former British
and Netherlands territories, which, if culturally distinct, yet
have much geographically, economically, politically and
socially in common with their Spanish and French speaking
neighbours. French Canada, on the other hand, is nowadays
implicitly excluded.

We may therefore define the coverage of this work as 'all
the Americas, south of the Rio Grande (including the adjacent
islands from Bermuda across to Easter Island and down to
the Falkland Island Dependencies), plus the Spanish speaking
areas and minority groups within the United States.'

Be warned, however, that usage of this and similar terms
varies considerably, and never make assumptions about the
coverage of a reference source from its title. 'Hispanic
America' is a particular trap: for many writers it is synon-
ymous with 'Spanish America', whilst for others it includes
Brazil. The use of 'Indian', 'West Indian' and 'British West
Indies' can also mislead.

General reference sources versus regional ones

A constant problem in compiling a guide of this sort is deci-
ding how far one should restrict it to sources solely concerned with 'Latin America', and how far one should remind the
reader of the Latin American coverage of more general
works.

Clearly no one is going to hunt up the Barbados census to
find the sum total of the island's population if he has
Whitaker's Almanack at hand, nor will he seek out a

General reference sources versus regional ones (cont'd.)

Mexican source for the address of that country's national
university when he can look it up in the current World of
learning. Sometimes indeed the general work may provide
the best answer even to a detailed enquiry: see, for instance,
the information on the Brazilian Vil(l)a Lobos contained in
Grove's Dictionary of music and musicians (due to be re-
edited, Spring 1979, as The new Grove dictionary).

Attempting, however, to discuss the Latin American coverage of even the most frequently used general reference
sources would merely duplicate information readily available in such guides as Albert J.Walford's Guide to reference material (3.ed., London, The Library Association, 3
vols, 1973-77), Eugene P.Sheehy's Guide to reference books
(9.ed., Chicago, American Library Association, 1976) or
Louise N.Malclès' Sources du travail bibliographique (Geneva, Droz, 3 vols, 1950-58) and her Manuel de bibliographie
(3.ed., Paris, Presses Universitaires de France, 1976).

We do from time to time make mention of such general
sources, usually where there is no adequate Latin American
substitute, but normally we restrict ourselves to the specifically Latin American, trusting the student will know of
general sources already, or will be able easily to find out
about them elsewhere.

Contrariwise, we generally avoid mentioning works and
sources whose coverage is limited to a single country (or
smaller area); to enumerate these would bulk our material
twentyfold.

We should also stress that this work is an initial guide, not
a fully comprehensive bibliography. Our object has been,
wherever possible, to direct you to an appropriate and rea-
sonably accessible source that would itself pursue each
topic in depth; we have gone into detail only where no such
source seemed available or adequate.

A note on coverage

Accuracy and partiality

Even Homer nods, and even lexicographers have had axes to grind. The bibliographer can only provide you with a list. Although he may venture to omit some of the most notoriously untrustworthy sources, or point out the most blatant cases of bias (ideological or other), do not expect him to do your work of evaluation for you. And take care not to accept repetition as evidence of truth: inaccuracies are all too often perpetuated through whole generations of reference works.

Be, nonetheless, compassionate towards the compilers of reference books. So very often the faults in a work are, particularly in a Latin American context, the inevitable result of attempting more than could be achieved with the time, the personnel or the funds available, or in the prevailing political or social conditions.

INTRODUCTION

Purpose

Courses in Latin American bibliography - by which we mean the systematic study of sources of information and research on the region - are an integral part of at least the graduate programmes in Latin American studies at most major North American universities. In the British Isles, as yet, they are almost unknown.

The range of material with which the researcher needs to become acquainted is considerable. Basic facts can be ascertained from encyclopaedias and handbooks. A plethora of bibliographies - general, national and subject - provides access to the mass of printed books, and may be supplemented by library catalogues, many of which have been published. There are indexes of periodical articles, and guides to special types of material, such as newspapers and manuscripts. Directories and biographical dictionaries inform about institutions and personalities. Non-book sources include data banks and research organisations.

We do not pretend to substitute adequately for a course of instruction. We do, however, hope to provide some initial orientation in the field, and reduce some of the newcomer's frustrations.

Unfortunately not everything we recommend can be provided in every library, but there will frequently be substitutes that the staff can suggest to you. Remember it is their job to help, and they are frequently your best source of information, particularly regarding the latest publications and developments.

Arrangement

We have sought to facilitate reference by a strictly alphabetic ordering of the topics we cover. As may be seen from the contents list, these are forms of material, and categories of information sources, rather than specific subjects.

Arrangement (cont'd.)

Adequate treatment of individual subjects is beyond the scope
of a book this size, although we do attempt in the section on
'SUBJECT BIBLIOGRAPHY' to make a few general remarks
on major subject areas.

Your attention is particularly directed to the sections 'LIB-
RARY FACILITIES' and 'CATALOGUES & INDEXES'.
Those planning to read the entire book are invited to begin
with these, and follow them, in turn, with 'BIBLIOGRAPH-
IES', 'PRINTED CATALOGUES', 'INTER-LIBRARY LEN-
DING' and 'BRITISH UNION CATALOGUE OF LATIN-
AMERICANA'.

Introductory material

There are two kinds of books that will interest those first en-
tering the field of Latin American studies: reference works,
to provide quick access to basic facts, and discursive works
offering a general view of one area or subject.

Basic reference works are discussed in the sections 'DIREC-
TORIES', 'ENCYCLOPAEDIAS' and 'HANDBOOKS AND
GUIDES'. Discursive works on particular countries we treat
below; those on particular subjects are mentioned in the section 'SUBJECT BIBLIOGRAPHY'. For a completely general
introduction you might consider:

> Véliz, Claudio, ed.: Latin America and the Carib-
> bean, a handbook. (London, Blond, 1968) - short
> articles by various contributors on each country
> in various subject sections;

> Reed, Irving B., and others: The Latin American
> scene of the 'seventies: a basic fact book. (Coral
> Gables, Center for advanced international studies
> of the University of Miami, 1972).

Introduction

Introductions to specific countries

Most countries have been covered (and second editions have appeared for many) in the Area handbook series produced by Foreign Area Studies of the American University, Washington D.C., for the United States Army. These contain general information on the history, geography, economy and culture of each country, as well as a section on its armed forces.

In the 1950's and 1960's the Royal Institute of International Affairs issued, in conjunction with the Oxford University Press, a series of general introductions that included Argentina, Paraguay and Uruguay (all by George Pendle), Bolivia (by Harold Osborne), British Guiana (by Raymond T. Smith), British Honduras (by David A.G. Waddell), the Central American republics (by Franklin D. Parker), Colombia (by William O. Galbraith), Ecuador (by Lilo Linke), Mexico (by Howard F. Cline), Peru (by Ronald J. Owens) and Venezuela (by Edwin Lieuwen). British Honduras and British Guiana were also included, together with Jamaica, in HMSO's Corona library series.

The Board of Trade and its successors have long issued brief, but regularly updated, Hints to businessmen pamphlets, which have been published for all the countries of the area.

Space precludes listing the many further works that exist, but these may easily be traced in library catalogues, or through the sources listed in our section on 'NATIONAL BIBLIOGRAPHY'.

Authorship

This work was initiated by the Latin American Group of SCONUL (the Standing Conference of National and University Libraries), and has drawn on the contributions and advice of many persons: members of the Group and of the Committee on Latin America, librarians from the British

Introduction

Authorship   (cont'd.)

Library, from the principal Latin American library collections in this country and from a number of other libraries, and members of the Society for Latin American Studies. The editor owes a particular debt of gratitude to Peter Johnson, Latin American bibliographer at the University of Minnesota.

The principal contributors are named on the titlepage, and also have their initials at the end of any section for which they were primarily or largely responsible.

The editorial work was begun by the then secretary of the SCONUL Latin American Group, Bernard Naylor, and completed by his successor, Laurence Hallewell.

As the work of editing has involved extensive rewriting, both to avoid overlapping treatment of the same topic and to take advantage of comments received as the work progressed, the final wording is the editor's sole responsibility, and the presence of a contributor's initials does not necessarily indicate his or her approval of all the preceding text. Nor should any views expressed be in any wise attributed to SCONUL.

Acknowledgments

Most of the preparatory work was done while the editor was Latin American librarian at the University of Essex and he is much indebted to the support and encouragement he received from his colleagues there, particularly the Librarian, Philip Long.

Printing and binding has been ably and most efficiently carried out by the Support Section and Print Room staff of the School of Oriental and African Studies.

Finally, publication has been made possible by a generous grant from the Institute of Latin American Studies of the University of London.

L. Hallewell - February 1978

ABBREVIATIONS & ACRONYMS

Dictionaries of abbreviations

Latin Americans in general (and perhaps Brazilians in particular) seem to be even more enamoured of acronyms than the rest of us, and their use is seldom accompanied by any explanation. The following dictionaries of abbreviations will help with the commoner ones. Unfortunately, new ones crop up all the time and the student will be well advised to keep his own file of those relevant to his field of interest.

> United Nations. Economic commission for Latin America: Lista de siglas latinoamericanas/Latin American initialisms and acronyms, with English translations. (Santiago de Chile, Biblioteca de la CEPAL, 1970; reprinted, Detroit, Ethridge, 1974) - Latin American regional and national organisations only; only official translations given;

> United States Joint publications research service: Abbreviations in the Latin American press. (New York, CCM Information Corporation, 1972);

> Romaña, José María de: Diccionario de siglas. (Lima, the author?, 1973) - world wide abbreviations list with "suplemento latinoamericano";

> Fitzgibbon, Russel H.: A directory of Latin American political parties. (Tempe, Center for Latin American studies of Arizona State University, 1970) - includes a most useful list of abbreviations of party names;

> Lorscheiter, Vendelino: Siglas e abreviaturas. (Tokyo, Centro de estudos luso-brasileiros da Universidade Sofia, 1971) - mainly from Brazil and Portugal, but some from Spanish America;

> Instituto brasileiro de bibliografia e documentação: Siglas brasileiras: dicionário de entidades e publicações. (Rio de Janeiro, Serviço de publicações do IBBD, 1975) - 2.ed. of a 1970

Abbreviations & acronyms

Dictionaries of abbreviations (cont'd.)

work by Marilena de Castro França and
W. de Almeida. Limited to Brazilian organisations, but includes their addresses.

Other sources

Library catalogues sometimes include references from
organisations' acronyms to their full titles, and many
reference books contain short lists. The commoner abbreviations are often explained in appendices to language
dictionaries.

Acronyms in the fields of education, publishing, bibliography
and librarianship are listed in the SALALM Newsletter 3(3),
March 1976, pp.40-43, and later issues.

There is also an index of acronyms maintained in a card file
at the library of the London Institute of Latin American
Studies (31, Tavistock Square, WC1H 9HA - 'phone:
01-387-4055).

[LH]

AUDIO-VISUAL MATERIAL

Definition

The term 'audio-visual' embraces cinematic films, film-strips, slides, photographs, pictorial packages (e.g. Jackdaw publications) and recorded sound (on tapes or discs). It is not usually employed to cover document reproduction by microphotography (microfilms etc.): this we treat separately under 'MICROFORM MATERIAL'.

In the British Isles

There is quite a wealth of audio-visual material in the country that could interest the Latin Americanist, but it is scattered, much of it in collections that are not directly concerned with regional studies at all. Nor is it all housed in libraries; at the University of Essex, for instance, the Art Department collects slides on pre-Colombian art and there is an archive of recordings of Brazilian poetry in the Language Department. Note that the British Library Lending Division acquires only mixed-media presentations where part of the mix is a printed work.

As no adequate guides exist, you will have to depend a lot on the personal knowledge (and intuition) of your own library's staff, and on that of your lecturers and fellow students, as to where to search. Some assistance may be obtained from mention of audio-visual resources in some of the entries in:

> Naylor, Bernard, and others: Directory of libraries and special collections on Latin America and the West Indies. (London, The Athlone Press, 1975).

Consult also the sections 'Media' and 'Photography' (pp.10-13 & 66) of:

> Great Britain. Science reference library: Guide to government department and other libraries and information bureaux. (London, British Library, 1976).

In the British Isles (cont'd.)

There has been an attempt to list what has been published in this country, but this has been done primarily with the needs of secondary and primary school teaching in mind:

> Hunt, Rosemary: Latin America, a critical analysis of teaching materials. (London, the Voluntary Committee on Overseas Aid and Development, 1974) - useful, critical commentary, and list of publishers specialising in the audio-visual field.

If you wish to hire films from, or about, Latin America, whether feature or documentary (16mm or larger), the best sources in this country are probably the British Film Institute (81 Dean Street, London W1V 6AA) and "The Other Cinema" (25 Tottenham Street, London W1). You could also approach the cultural attachés of the various embassies and high commissions: the Brazilian embassy (32 Green Street, London W1Y 4AT) has a large selection available on loan.

In North America

Although of limited use to the U.K. student, there is a bibliography similar in conception to Hunt, aimed at U.S. college students:

> Loy, Jane M.: Latin America, sights and sounds: a guide to motion pictures and music for college students. (Gainesville FL, The Consortium of Latin American studies programs [CLASP], 1973).

Films (whether of American or foreign origin) are also covered in a special sectional catalogue of the Library of Congress, Films (and other materials for projection), an annual since 1948 (with some changes of title during that period). It is arranged by title, with a subject index, and is cumulated about every four years.

Audio-visual material

In North America (cont'd.)

A useful bibliography, giving U.S. sources for Latin American films, is:

> Burton, Julianne: The new Latin American cinema: a annotated bibliography of English language sources, 1960-1976. (New York, Cineaste Magazine, 1976) - despite the subtitle, this includes some Spanish, Portuguese and French material.

The Library of Congress has been building up a collection of recorded readings by Latin American and Peninsular authors of their own poems and other works, since 1942. There are currently some 350 writers included, in Catalan, French, Nahuatl, Portuguese, Quechua, Spanish and Zapotec. Copies of the tapes may be purchased by 'non-profit institutions' from the Music Division, Recorded Sound Section, Library of Congress, Washington DC 20540. A selection of the Archive is being made available on LP records for purchase by the general public, although only four have been issued so far. For details of the Archive, see:

> Aguilera, Francisco, and Dorn, G.M.: Guide to the Archive of Hispanic literature on tape. (Washington, GPO, 1974, and Supplement, 1977).

A guide to collections of audio-visual material, which is intended to include the British Isles as well as North America, is being compiled by the Seminar on the Acquisition of Latin American Library Materials (SALALM). Eventual publication (date unknown) will be by the SALALM Secretariat at the Benson Library of the University of Texas at Austin.

In the West Indies

A useful article on the recorded music of the English-, French- and Dutch-speaking Caribbean, which has notes on library collections in the U.K. and elsewhere, and has information on record companies:

Audio-visual material

In the West Indies (cont'd.)

> Bloomfield, Valerie: "Caribbean recordings:
> notes on sources, with a select discography",
> Journal of librarianship, 8(1), Jan. 1976,
> pp. 47-72.

This may be supplemented, in the case of Barbados and
Guyana, by reference to the respective national bibliographies
(see: 'NATIONAL BIBLIOGRAPHY'): these two are at present
about the only countries in either the West Indies or Latin
America where new records are systematically listed in the
national bibliography.

Mrs. Bloomfield has also written on documentary and feature
film production in the Commonwealth Caribbean:

> Bloomfield, Valerie: "Caribbean films", Journal
> of librarianship, 9(4), Oct. 1977, pp. 278-314 -
> includes bibliography and select filmography.

In Latin America

Books of poetry and other literary works are sometimes
issued with accompanying records of the text, in Latin
America as elsewhere. Such publications appear in new book
lists and other bibliographies (see: 'BOOKS & PAMPHLETS'
and 'NATIONAL BIBLIOGRAPHY'), and they are available
through normal booktrade channels (see: 'BOOKSELLERS').

Recorded music is more difficult to obtain. Discs of popular
music are easily bought on the spot in the larger towns of
Latin America, and popularised Indian music is readily available, especially in Argentina and Mexico. It is not easy to
come by recordings of serious and classical music by local
composers, or of genuine Amerindian or other folkmusic, even
if you visit the countries concerned. Such recordings do exist,
but they are issued in tiny editions that soon sell out. There
are instances of Amerindian music being recorded by foreign
investigators and published abroad, as for example B. Moser
and D. Tayler's The music of some Indian tribes of Colombia

Audio-visual material

In Latin America (cont'd.)

(three LP discs with text and photographs) issued by the British Institute of Recorded Sound in 1973.

A Spanish American bookseller interested in selling records to his overseas customers - he has a regular listing in his catalogues - is:

> ODDLA (Organización difusora del libro americano)
> Casilla de correos 557,
> Montevideo, Uruguay.

Bibliographies of national film production exist for Brazil, Mexico and other countries, but the only general listing (apart from the Library of Congress and Burton catalogues already mentioned) is:

> Mitry, Jean: Bibliographie internationale du cinéma et de la télévision. Section 3: Espagne, Portugal et pays de langue espagnole et portugaise. (Paris, Institut des Hautes études cinématographiques, 1968).

London record shops

The following West End shops stock records of Latin American music:

> Collets Record Shop, 180 Shaftesbury Avenue, WC2;

> Discurio International Record Store, 9 Shepherd Street, W1;

> EMI Records, 363 Oxford Street, W1.

[BMH]

AUTHOR & PERSONAL BIBLIOGRAPHY

Library catalogues

Any major library catalogue will provide an author bibliography, that is. works by an author issued as separate publications. The United States National Union Catalog is
noteworthy, not only for its comprehensiveness, but because
it usually includes an author's birth and death dates in its
headings, and often has a footnote giving full legal form of
his name.

The so-called 'dictionary catalogue' favoured by American
libraries will also give, under a person's name (usually
following a list of any books by him) a list of separately
published works about him, including any published bibliographies. (For information on such catalogues as have been
published, see the section 'PRINTED CATALOGUES').

Normal British practice is to have separate 'author' and
'subject' catalogues, and logically you might expect books
and bibliographies about a person to be listed in the latter.
In most cases, however, they are listed in the author file
(following any works by the person), which is then known in
library jargon as a 'name catalogue'. Find out before
searching just what your library's practice is in the matter.

Using bibliographies of bibliographies

We know of no comprehensive guide specifically on Latin
American personal bibliography, and international lists never
seem to cover any but the most widely known figures from
the region: Max Arnim's International Personalbiblio-
graphie, for instance, lacks mention of Borges, Benito
Juárez and Machado de Assis. We suggest using instead the
works listed under "Bibliographies of bibliographies" in our
section 'BIBLIOGRAPHIES - GENERAL'. Gropp, mentioned there, has an extensive section 'Biography (individual)'. Important, particularly for works too recent for Gropp,
are the annual volumes of the Handbook of Latin American
Studies (search under the person's name in the subject index
of each volume). Several of the works we refer to under

Author & personal bibliography

Using bibliographies of bibliographies (cont'd.)

'NATIONAL BIBLIOGRAPHY' are indexed in ways that permit author and personal bibliographies to be traced.

Using biographies and biographical dictionaries etc.

Not only will any good biography contain a relevant bibliography, but the articles in biographical dictionaries, such as those we discuss under 'BIOGRAPHICAL INFORMATION' will often list their subject's published books and articles, and occasionally works about him too.

Do not overlook a writer's own works as a source of information about him. A list of his "other publications" is frequently included in the preliminary matter (often facing the title page or on its verso). Latin American publishers are particularly fond of providing biographical detail about their authors, usually on the back cover, but sometimes elsewhere in the book.

Literary bio-bibliography: Spanish American authors

Personal bibliography is most needed in the field of literary authorship, which is just where reference books cater best. Nevertheless the most comprehensive guide to biographical and bibliographical information on Spanish American men of letters remains a work that is now forty years old:

> Grismer, Raymond L.: A reference index to twelve thousand Spanish American authors ... (New York, Wilson, 1939, reprinted New York, Franklin, 1970, and Detroit, Ethridge, 1971).

More recent, but much more restricted in its range is:

> Bryant, Shasta M.: A selected bibliography of bibliographies of Hispanic American literature. (Washington, Division of philosophy and letters of the Pan American Union, 1966) - index includes names of the subjects of personal bibliographies.

Literary bio-bibliography: Spanish American authors

There are well annotated sections on Spanish American literary figures in:

Foster, David W., and Foster, Virginia Ramos: Manual of Hispanic bibliography. (Seattle, University of Washington Press, 1970);

Bleznick, Donald W.: A sourcebook for Hispanic language and literature: a selected, annotated guide to Spanish and Spanish American bibliography, literature, linguistics, journals and other source material. (Philadelphia, Temple University Press, 1974).

A recent, comprehensive work which includes periodical articles, is:

Flores, Ángel: Bibliografía de escritores hispanoamericanos/A bibliography of Spanish American writers, 1609-1974. (New York, Gordian, 1975).

For contemporary novelists there is:

Foster, David W.: The Twentieth-century Spanish American novel: a bibliographic guide. (Metuchen, Scarecrow, 1975).

Apart from these, one has to fall back on biographical dictionaries with good bibliographies. One of the most important is the never completed

Pan American Union. Division of philosophy and letters: Diccionario de la literatura latinoamericana. (Washington, the Union, 6 vols in 8, 1958-63) - only the volumes for Argentina, Bolivia, Central America, Chile, Colombia and Ecuador were ever published; the first two volumes were issued by the then Letters Section of the Division of philosophy, letters and sciences.

Author & personal bibliography

A still useful work (the first edition came out in 1816-21)
is:

> Beristain de Souza, José Mariano: Biblioteca
> hispanoamericana septentrional; o, catálogo
> y noticias de los literatos que o nacidos o edu-
> cados o florecientes en la America septentrio-
> nal española, han dado a luz algún escrito ...
> 1521-1850, 3.ed.   (Mexico City, Fuente
> Cultural, 8 vols in 4, 1947-51).

Living writers are covered in:

> Foster, David W.: A dictionary of contem-
> porary Latin American authors.   (Tempe,
> Center for Latin American studies of
> Arizona State University, 1975) - and:

> Ocampo de Gómez, Aurora Maura: Novelis-
> tas iberoamericanos contemporáneos.
> (Mexico City, Centro de estudios literarios
> de la UNAM, 1971-   ) - in progress.

An alternative source is any good general history of Spanish
American literature. There are many of these, but the most
easily consulted (and one of the most comprehensive) for
information on individual authors, is probably:

> Anderson-Imbert, Enrique: Historia de la
> literatura hispanoamericana, 4.ed.
> (Mexico City, Fondo de cultura económica,
> 2 vols, 1962-64).

These may be supplemented by many works on individual
countries (see: 'NATIONAL BIBLIOGRAPHY').

Author & personal bibliography

<u>Literary bio-bibliography: Brazilian authors</u>

The standard bibliography of Brazilian literature is by Carpeaux (known to some library catalogues by the original form of his name, Karpfeu):

> Carpeaux, Otto Maria: <u>Pequena bibliografia crítica de literatura brasileira</u>, 2.ed. (Rio de Janeiro, Serviço de documentação do Ministério da educação e cultura, 1955, reprinted Ouro, 1971).

A briefer work is:

> Topete, José Manuel: <u>A working bibliography of Brazilian literature.</u> (Gainesville, University of Florida Press, 1957).

More information, especially on less prominent authors, will be found in a biographical dictionary by Menezes which has good bibliographies:

> Menezes, Raimundo de: <u>Dicionário literário brasileiro ilustrado.</u> (São Paulo, Saraiva, 5 vols, 1969).

Older writers can be found in:

> Blake, Augusto Victorino Alves Sacramento: <u>Diccionario bibliographico brazileiro.</u> (Rio de Janeiro, Imprensa nacional for the author, 7 vols, 1883-1902, reprinted, Nendeln, Kraus, 1969).

<u>Literary bio-bibliography: West-Indian authors</u>

> Alleyne, Alvona: "Preliminary check-list of literary works published in Jamaica 1900-1976" in her "Literary publishing in the English-speaking Caribbean", <u>Twenty-first Seminar on the Acquisition of Latin American Library Materials,</u> Bloomington (Ind.), 1976 (Working paper B-9);

Author & personal bibliography

Literary bio-bibliography: West-Indian authors (cont'd.)

Barbados Public Library: Our common heritage: authors among us. (Bridgetown, the Library, 1971);

Jones, Joseph J., and Jones, Johanna: Authors and areas of the West Indies. (Austin, Speck-Vaughn, 1970);

Merriman, Stella E., and Christiani, Joan: Commonwealth Caribbean writers: a bibliography. (Georgetown, Public Free Library, 1970);

Pantin, Maritza, and Hunte, Diane: Creative writers in Trinidad and Tobago, a bibliography. (St. Augustine, Library of the Trinidad campus of the University of the West Indies, 1970) – works by and about; includes reviews and periodical articles.

Anonyms and pseudonyms

Medina, José Toribio: Diccionario de anónimos y seudónimos hispanoamericanos. (Buenos Aires, Imprenta de la Universidad, 1925, plus 2 vols of corrections and additions by Ricardo Victorica, 1928-29, all three volumes being reprinted, Detroit, Ethridge, 1973);

Scarone, Arturo: Apuntes para un diccionario de seudónimos y publicaciones anónimas, 2.ed. (Montevideo, 1934).

These can be supplemented by works on individual literatures, such as those of Cutolo and Durán on Argentine pseudonyms, Pérez Ortiz on those of Colombia, and Scarone on those of Uruguay.

[PN]

BIBLIOGRAPHIES - GENERAL

Range and type of material

This section deals only with the most general guides. Immediately below we list bibliographies of bibliographies on the region - books about books about books in fact. These are followed by straightforward bibliographies (mere books about books), but only those which try to cover the whole region in all subject fields, and unrestricted by language. (Guides which are restricted to material in particular languages are dealt with in the sections 'BIBLIOGRAPHIES - HISPANIC LANGUAGE MATERIAL', 'BIBLIOGRAPHIES - MATERIAL IN OTHER LANGUAGES').

Few bibliographers can cope adequately with the literature of so vast an area in a single work, and much better coverage can usually be found in the various specialised bibliographies. These we deal with elsewhere. Guides to special forms of material are treated under the heading appropriate to each: 'LAW & LEGISLATION', 'MAPS & ATLASES', 'MUSIC', 'NEWS & CURRENT AFFAIRS', 'OFFICIAL PUBLICATIONS', 'PERIODICALS' and 'THESES' are examples. Bibliographies covering the whole region but limited to particular subjects are in the section 'SUBJECT BIBLIOGRAPHY'. Works on the book- and periodical- production of specific countries, and also bibliographies of works about specific countries, are discussed under 'NATIONAL BIBLIOGRAPHY'. Bibliographies about individuals and their works will be found under 'AUTHOR & PERSONAL BIBLIOGRAPHY'. Finally, if you just want the title of a book that will give you a broad general introduction to a major discipline or area of study, you will find our suggestions under 'SUBJECT BIBLIOGRAPHY - MAJOR SUBJECTS'.

Bibliographies of bibliographies

A recent listing by subject is:

> Cordeiro, Daniel R.: "A bibliography of Latin
> American bibliographies", Twenty-first
> Seminar on the Acquisition of Latin American
> Library Materials, Bloomington (Ind.), 1976
> (Working paper A-2) - this continues the an-
> nual SALALM "Report on bibliographical
> activities" intended to supplement:

> Gropp, Arthur E.: A bibliography of Latin
> American bibliographies. (Metuchen,
> Scarecrow, 1968, plus supplement covering
> 1965-69, in 1971) - by subject, subarranged
> by country, and itself claimed to be an up-
> dating of:

> Jones, Cecil K.: A bibliography of Latin
> American bibliographies, 2.ed. (Washington,
> GPO, 1942, reprinted New York, Greenwood,
> 1969) - by country, subarranged by subject,
> critically annotated.

An Argentine contribution is:

> Geogheghan, Abel Rodolfo: Obras de referencia
> de América latina: repertorio selectivo y ano-
> tado de enciclopedias, diccionarios, bibliogra-
> fías ... (Buenos Aires, Crisol, 1965).

Another Argentine work which has excellent Latin American
coverage, although it is not limited to the region is:

> Sabor, Josefa Emilia: Manual de fuentes de infor-
> mación: obras de referencia, enciclopedias, dic-
> cionarios, bibliografías, biografías etc. (Buenos
> Aires, Kapelusz, 1957; enlarged 2.ed., 1967).

Bibliographies - general

Comprehensive bibliographies

'Comprehensive' is used here to mean coverage of the entire region without restriction as to subject: all the works listed will inevitably be selective to a greater or lesser degree.

> American Universities Field Staff: A select bibliography: Asia, Africa, Eastern Europe, Latin America. (New York, AUFS, 1960, with supplements in 1961 and alternate years thereafter) - Latin American section arranged by country, subarranged by subject;

> Berliner (J.J.) and Staff: Bibliography of Latin America 1935-1940. (New York, the Berliner organisation, 1941);

> Dillon, Dorothy R.: Latin America, 1935-1949: a selected bibliography. (New York, United Nations, 1952);

> Estep, Raymond: A Latin American bibliography. (Maxwell Air Force Base, Documentary research division of Aerospace Studies Institution, 1969) - post-1960 publications, by country, subarranged by subject; mainly economics, politics and history;

> North American Congress on Latin America: NACLA's bibliography on Latin America. (New York, NACLA, 1973) - leftist;

> Sable, Martin Howard: A guide to Latin American studies. (Los Angeles, Latin American Center of UCLA, 1967) - classified, with author and subject indexes;

> United States of America. Defense documentation center: Latin America: a bibliography. (Alexandria, Va., Cameron Station, 1965).

Bibliographies - general

Lists of 'essential works'

Somewhat narrower in scope are listings of 'essential works' for basic library collections, high schools etc. Such are:

> Levy, Kurt L.: Book list on Latin America for Canadians ... (Ottawa, Canadian Commission for UNESCO, 1969);

> Pariseau, Earl J., ed.: Latin America, an acquisition guide for colleges and public libraries. (Washington, Consortion of Latin American Studies Programs [CLASP], 1975);

> Wilgus, Karna S.: Latin America books, an annotated bibliography for high schools and colleges. (New York, Center for Inter-American Relations, 1974).

Keeping up to date

The Jones-Gropp-Cordeiro series are updated by a "Report on bibliographic activities" which is one of the papers in each SALALM annual conference, although it is not available, except to participants, until a year or more after presentation. This is in turn supplemented by listings of new bibliographies (very comprehensively covered) in:

> SALALM Newsletter. (Austin, Texas, Secretariat of the Seminar on the Acquisition of Latin American Library Materials, January 1973-   ) - published two to three times a year.

Apart from this and the AUFS work with its regular supplements, all the works we have mentioned are restricted to what existed at the time they were first compiled. The serious student needs to keep aware of what is currently being published. The most important current bibliography is the:

Keeping up to date (cont'd.)

> Handbook of Latin American studies, 1935-
> (Cambridge, Mass., etc., 1936-55; Gainesville,
> University of Florida Press for the Library of
> Congress, 1957-   ) - each of the earlier
> volumes tried to cover a year's publications,
> but since vol 27 the work has alternated be-
> tween "Social sciences" and "Humanities"
> volumes, each one covering (in theory) the
> publications of the previous two years; in
> practice, entries tend, by time of actual pub-
> lication, to be 3 to 5 years old. Arrangement
> is by broad subject, with (in recent years) full
> indexes of subjects (including persons) and of
> authors (including titles of anonymous works
> and periodicals) in each issue. There is a
> separately published cumulated author index
> for vols 1-28. European works, as well as
> those from the Americas, are well covered,
> and periodical articles are included. Good
> annotation.

Most serious journals will also list, and usually review,
important bibliographies in their subject field: see our
section 'BOOK REVIEWS'.

Bibliographies appearing in periodicals

Most (but not all) of the above limit themselves to separately published works. A recent guide to bibliographies
appearing in periodicals is:

> Gropp, Arthur E.: A bibliography of Latin American
> bibliographies published in periodicals. (Metuchen,
> Scarecrow, 2 vols, 1976) - arranged by discipline or
> field, subarranged by country. Nearly 10,000 entries
> from several hundred journals.

[LH]

BIBLIOGRAPHIES -
HISPANIC LANGUAGE MATERIAL

List of 'essential works'

Woodbridge, Hensley C., and Newberry, D., eds.:
Basic list of Latin American materials in
Spanish, Portuguese and French. (Amherst,
Mass., SALALM, 1975) - annotated.

Books in print

The Bowker Company of New York, publishers of the annual
Books in print in the American booktrade, also produce a
decennial Spanish language equivalent, currently issued from
their Buenos Aires office:

Libros en venta en Hispanoamérica y España.
(New York, Bowker, 1964, with 4 "suplementos"
issued in Buenos Aires by Bowker Argentina,
covering books published during 1964-71; 2.ed.,
Buenos Aires, 1974, covering books in print in
1972, with later [annual?] "suplementos") - lists
by author, by title, and by subjects classified
according to the Dewey Decimal Classification
used in public libraries.

The Sindicato nacional dos editores de livros (SNEL) issued
a list of books in print in Brazil, Edições brasileiras in
1963, with supplements in 1964 and 1965, but there has been
no attempt to produce anything similar since.

Current publications

Bowker also originated the Fichero bibliográfico hispanoamericano, a companion work to Libros en venta. This lists
new books by subject according to the Dewey Decimal Classification, with indexes of authors and titles. There are also
lists of publishers, feature articles of interest to the booktrade and to librarians, notably "Lecturas profesionales"
reviewing new reference books. Early each year 'Noticias
anticipadas" lists titles announced for future publication,

Bibliographies - Hispanic language material

Current publications (cont'd.)

arranged by publisher. The Fichero began in October 1961,
in New York, as a quarterly; in October 1964 it was transferred to Buenos Aires, since when it has appeared eleven
times a year. Present publishers are Turner Ediciones
SRL. Like the related Libros en venta, it does not include
books from Brazil, or the Commonwealth Caribbean countries, except for occasional brief lists of "Libros del
Brasil" thought likely to interest booksellers in Spanish
America.

In 1974 UNESCO's Centro regional para el fomento del libro
en América latina, in Bogotá, inaugurated its Boletín bibliográfico CERLAL, which is similar in coverage to Fichero,
and is also a monthly. It is important for official, academic
and other non-commercial publications which the booktrade-
orientated Fichero tends to overlook.

Sources of information on new Brazilian publications are set
out in the section 'BOOKS & PAMPHLETS', in the paragraph 'New books in Portuguese'.

Retrospective lists: Spanish

Catálogo general de la librería española e his-
panoamericana, años 1901-1930. (Madrid,
Instituto nacional del libro español, 5 vols,
1932-51, plus supplement by F. Zamora Lucas
covering 1931-1950, 4 vols, 1957-65);

Comité organizador del trigésimo Congreso internacional de Americanistas: Biblioteca american-
ista española 1935-1963. (Seville, 1964);

Medina, José Toribio: Biblioteca hispanoameri-
cana 1493-1810. (Santiago de Chile, the author,
7 vols, 1898-1907; reprinted Amsterdam, Israel,
1962) - 8500 titles arranged chronologically;

Retrospective lists: Spanish (cont'd.)

> Palau y Dulcet, Antonio: Manual del librero
> hispanoamericano: bibliografía general
> española e hispanoamericana desde la in-
> vención de la imprenta hasta nuestros tiem-
> pos, 2.ed. (Barcelona, the author, 1948-) -
> in progress but almost completed, arranged
> by author.

Retrospective lists: Portuguese

The standard guide to Brazilian bibliography is:

> Moraes, Rubens Borba Alves de, and Berrien,W.:
> Manual bibliográfico de estudos brasileiros.
> (Rio de Janeiro, Souza, 1949).

An account of the development of Brazilian bibliography
which will also indicate sources too recent for inclusion in
Moraes is:

> Hallewell, Laurence: "The development of
> national bibliography in Brazil", Libri
> 23(4), Oct.1973, pp.291-297.

National lists

The foregoing should be supplemented, in the case of
Spanish America, by bibliographies of the individual
countries. These are discussed in the section 'NATIONAL
BIBLIOGRAPHY'.

[LH]

BIBLIOGRAPHIES - MATERIAL IN ENGLISH

Selective

A brief introductory list, now somewhat dated, is:

> Hispanic and Luso-Brazilian Councils: Latin America: an introduction to modern books in English concerning the countries of Latin America, 2.ed. (London, The Library Association, 1966).

A regularly revised list of paperbacks in print is:

> Dorn, Georgette M.: Latin America, Spain and Portugal: an annotated bibliography of paperback books, 2.ed. (Washington, Library of Congress, 1976).

Retrospective

A list emphasising law and the social sciences:

> Bayitch, Stojan A.: Latin America and the Caribbean, a bibliographical guide to works in English. (Coral Gables, University of Miami Press, and, Dobbs Ferry, Oceana, 1967).

Slightly older, and emphasising history, but with much other material:

> Humphreys, Robert [alias Robin] A.: Latin American history: a guide to the literature in English. (London, Oxford University Press, 1958, reprinted 1960).

Bibliographies - material in English

There is also:

> Behrendt, Richard F.W.: Modern Latin America
> in social science literature: a selected, annotated
> bibliography of books, pamphlets and periodicals
> in English in the fields of economics, politics and
> sociology of Latin America. (Hamilton, NY, the
> author?, 1949, and supplement, Washington, Pan
> American Union, 1950).

Travellers' accounts make up much of:

> Naylor, Bernard: Accounts of nineteenth-century
> South America: an annotated checklist of works
> by British and United States observers. (London,
> Athlone Press, 1969).

None of these is very recent, but it is easy enough to extract
the English-language items from the more up-to-date bibliographies listed in our section 'BIBLIOGRAPHIES -
GENERAL'.

Current

A twice yearly listing of recent books and periodical articles
in English is:

> British bulletin of publications on Latin America,
> the West Indies, Portugal and Spain. (London,
> The Hispanic and Luso-Brazilian Council, 1949-   )
> - originally the Bulletin of British historical
> publications on ...

The Bulletin is, however, very selective. For a fuller (and
more frequently and more promptly published) list you would
need to consult the weekly British National Bibliography -
discussed in more detail in the section 'PRINTED CATA-
LOGUES' - for separately published items (via its monthly
subject index which includes geographical references), and
the quarterly British humanities index (under 'Latin

Current (cont'd.)

America' and individual countries) for periodical articles -
and then go on to consult similar general bibliographies and
indexes for the United States and other English-speaking
countries: see the paragraph 'New books in English' in our
section 'BOOKS & PAMPHLETS'.

Within two to three years of publication, however, almost all
of this material will be recorded by the Handbook of Latin
American Studies (see the last paragraph of the section
'BIBLIOGRAPHIES - GENERAL').

Translations

Clause L. Hulet has compiled two bibliographies of literary
translations, both published by the Pan American Union:
Latin American prose in English translation (1964) and
Latin American poetry in English translation (1965). Smaller but more recent is Suzanne J. Levine's Latin American
fiction and poetry in translation (New York, Center for
Inter-American Relations, 1971).

Claiming, however, to supplant all earlier work is:

> Shaw, Bradley A.: Latin American literature in
> English translation: an annotated bibliography.
> (New York, New York University Press, 1976).

The contents of 35 anthologies were indexed by Juan B.
Freudenthal and J. Katz in their "Preliminary index to
anthologized contemporary Latin American literature in
translation", working paper B-5 of the 20th SALALM, which
was later revised and published in book form by Freudenthal
and his wife as:

> Freudenthal, Juan B, and Freudenthal, Patricia M.:
> Index to anthologies of contemporary Latin
> American literature in English translation.
> (Boston, Hall, 1977).

Bibliographies - material in English

Translations (cont'd.)

There is also the Literatures of the world in English trans- lation: a bibliography, edited by George B. Parks and others, of which Vol 3, part one   (New York, Ungar, 1970) includes material from Spanish and Portuguese.

All these may be supplemented by UNESCO's annual inter- national Index translationum.

[LH]

BIBLIOGRAPHIES -
MATERIAL IN OTHER LANGUAGES

French

Lambert, Michel: Bibliographie latino-
américaniste, France, 1959-1972. (Mexico
City, Institut Français d'Amérique latine,
1973);

Woodbridge, Hensley C., and Newberry, D.,
eds.: Basic list of Latin American materials
in Spanish, Portuguese and French. (Amherst,
SALALM, 1975) - brief, annotated list of
'essential works'.

A list of 'Publications' appears in each issue of Cahiers
du monde hispanique et luso-brésilien (Toulouse, Univer-
sité de Toulouse, 1963-   , six-monthly), but a much
more complete listing can be obtained by checking the
international French bibliography Biblio (Paris, Hachette,
monthly with annual cumulations) under 'Amérique latine'.

Covering a year's output of the French-speaking Caribbean
(and, eventually, one hopes, to be continued) is:

Debien, Gabriel: "Antillas de lengua francesa,
1970-1971", Historiografía y bibliografía
americanistas, 16(2), Jly 1972, pp.257-314.

German

Palmer, Philip M.: German works on America,
1492-1800. (Berkeley, University of California
Press, 1952).

New German publications are announced in the Informationsdienst, Arbeitsgemeinschaft deutsche Latein-
amerikaforschung (Hamburg, FRG, 1966-   , quarterly),
and in Mundus, a quarterly review of German research on
Asia, Africa and Latin America (Stuttgart, Wissenschaft-
liche Verlagsgesellschaft, 1965-   ).

Bibliographies - material in other languages

Oriental, African and East European languages

Sable, Martin H.: Latin American studies in the non-western world and Eastern Europe: a bibliography on Latin America in the languages of Africa, Asia, the Middle East and Eastern Europe. (Metuchen, Scarecrow, 1970)

- and too recent for Sable:

Kula, Jan M.: "Polska literatura dotyczaca Ameryki Lacinskiej xix i xx w.", Dzieje nejnowsze rocznik (Warsaw), 4(4), 1972, pp.119-136;

Lidmilová, Pavla: "Bibliografia dos estudos luso-brasileiros de lingüística e de letras [de autores tchecos] 1945-1973", Ibero-Americana Pragensia, 7, 1974, pp.177-207.

Japanese

A retrospective catalogue of Japanese books on the area was issued in 1971 by the Kobe Diagaku Keizai Keikei Kenkyujo. More recently, the Sofia University's Instituto Iberoamericano in Tokyo published (in 1976) a Bibliografía de publicaciones japonesas sobre América latina, 1975, editado por Shiro Murae, (presumably) the first of an annual series.

Russian

The Institut Latinskoi Ameriki of the Soviet Academy of Sciences issues a regular Latinskaia Amerika v sovetskoi pechati, covering publications since 1946. The U.S. Library of Congress has been responsible for:

Okinshevich, Leo: Latin America in soviet writings: a bibliography, edited by Robert G. Carlton. (Baltimore, John Hopkins Press, 2 vols, 1966) - covers 1917 to 1964.

Bibliographies - material in other languages

Scandinavian languages

Benito, Miguel:Latinamerika i svensk biblio-
grafi/América latina en la bibliografía sueca,
1959-1969.   (Stockholm,Kungliga Biblioteket
& Latinamerika-Institutet, 1971).

This may be supplemented by the regular listings of new
Swedish publications in Ibero-Americana (Stockholm,
Latinamerika-Institutet, 1960-   , six-monthly), which
also includes works from Denmark, Finland and Norway.

[LH]

BIOGRAPHICAL INFORMATION

Biography of contemporaries

Sources of biographical information tend to divide themselves into those that limit themselves to living persons and
those that concentrate on the dead. We take the former first.

There is no satisfactory comprehensive source of biographical information covering Latin America and the West
Indies as a whole. The latest published dictionary of biography purporting to be comprehensive is:

> Dictionary of Latin American and Caribbean
> biography, general editor Ernest Kay, 2.ed.
> (London, Melrose, 1971) - a revision of his
> Dictionary of Caribbean biography (1970), and
> far from satisfactory for the rest of the region:
> a cursory check reveals no entries for Salvador
> Allende, Humberto Castelo Branco, Hector
> Campora, Gabriel García Márquez or Pablo
> Neruda.

An older work of contemporary biography that is still of use
is:

> Who's who in Latin America, a biographical dic-
> tionary of outstanding living men and women, 3.ed.,
> by Ronald Hilton. (Stanford, Cal., Stanford Uni-
> versity Press, 7 vols, 1946-52, reprinted Detroit,
> Ethridge, in 2 vols, 1971) - unlike the two earlier
> editions by Percy A. Martin in 1935 and 1940, this
> has a separate alphabetic sequence for each
> country, impeding reference if you do not know
> your subject's nationality.

For any contemporary Latin American or West Indian of
world stature (or world-wide newsworthiness) the best
source is probably an international directory, such as the
International who's who (40th ed., 1976/77) or the H.W.
Wilson Company's much more inclusive Current biography
(monthly since 1940, cumulating in regular Yearbooks,
decennially indexed). The newspaper indexes and news

Biographical information

Biography of contemporaries (cont'd.)

digests listed in our section 'NEWS & CURRENT AFFAIRS' will also prove rewarding: Keesing's contemporary archives, for instance, has a separate index of persons. These and Current biography are also good for obituaries, whilst the index to the New York Times was supplemented in 1970 by the publication of an Obituaries index 1858-1968.

Most countries also produce their own national Who's who, or Quién es quién, but few of these appear with any regularity. In Brazil, for example, Quem é quem came out in 1948, followed by eight later editions 1951-1967; In 1961, Afrânio Coutinho edited a similar compilation, Brasil e brasileiros de hoje, which was never republished; and then, in 1968, a new series began with the English title Who's who in Brazil. A second edition of this came out in 1970, and a third in 1971. Quién es quién en la Argentina (9 editions, 1939-1968, and a 'revised 9th edition' in 1969) seems to be the longest running of this type of publication in the region but it has now gone seven years without being up-dated.

Retrospective biography: bibliography

There is a Bibliography of the collective biography of Spanish America by Josefina del Toro (University of Puerto Rico, 1938), but this is now rather outdated. Slightly more recent information appears in the section on "Repertorios biográficos nacionales" in:

> Sabor, Josefa Emilia: Manual de fuentes de información. (Buenos Aires, Kapelusz, 1957).

The same author has also contributed:

> Sabor, Josefa Emilia: "Las fuentes biográficas para la República argentina", Bibliotecología (Buenos Aires), 3(1), Sep.1955, pp.3-12.

Biographical information

<u>Retrospective biography: bibliography</u> (cont'd.)

Sources for the countries of Gran Colombia may be found from:

Watson, Gayle H.: <u>Colombia, Ecuador and Venezuela: an annotated guide to reference materials ...</u> (Metuchen, Scarecrow, 1971).

Many retrospective biographical dictionaries for Brazil are listed in, and have a combined index provided for them by:

Sousa, José Galante de: <u>Índice de biobibliografia brasileira.</u> (Rio de Janeiro, Instituto nacional do livro, 1963).

Retrospective biography: collections

The best place to try first for retrospective biographies is probably any good encyclopaedia, especially one published in or about Latin America - see our section 'ENCYCLOPADEIAS'. The following may also be helpful:

Boyd-Bowman, Peter: <u>Índice geobiográfico de cuarenta mil pobladores españoles de América en el siglo dieciseis.</u> (Bogotá, Instituto Caro y Cuervo, 1964-   ) - in progress; volumes divided chronologically ;

Valcárcel Esparza, Carlos: <u>Biografías hispanoamericanas en el Archivo general de Indias.</u> (Lima, the author?, 1959).

The outstanding national biographical dictionaries are:

Cutolo, Vicente Osvaldo: <u>Nuevo diccionario biográfico argentino, 1750-1930.</u> (Buenos Aires, Elche, 1968-   ) - in progress;

<u>Diccionario biográfico de Chile, 16.ed.</u> (Santiago, Empresa periodística Chile, 1976);

Biographical information

Retrospective biography: collections (cont'd.)

Diccionario biográfico de México. (Mexico City, Revesa, 2 vols, 1968-1970);

Fernández Saldaña, José María: Diccionario uruguayo de biografías 1810-1940. (Montevideo, Amerindia, 1945);

Mendiburu, Manuel de: Diccionario histórico-biográfico del Perú, 2.ed. (Lima, Gil, 11 vols, 1931-35, plus "apéndice" by Evaristo San Cristoval, 1935-38).

Other sources

Space precludes our listing further sources, which range from the collected biography of a few leading figures, such as Patricia Baum's Dictators of Latin America (New York, Putnam, 1972) to biographical dictionaries attempting comprehensive cover of a small specialised field - for example, the U.S. Central Intelligence Agency's 1974 Directory of personalities of the Cuban government. We have indicated possible ways to trace such material in the sections 'BIBLIOGRAPHIES - GENERAL' (for general bibliographies of bibliographies), 'NATIONAL BIBLIO-GRAPHY' (for material on individual countries), 'SUBJECT BIBLIOGRAPHY' (for guides to study in particular subject fields), and 'AUTHOR & PERSONAL BIBLIOGRAPHY' (which lists material on literary figures and other writers).

Latin Americanists

Sources of information on academics and others involved in study and research on the region are given at the end of the section 'UNIVERSITY STUDY & RESEARCH'.

[PN]

BOOK REVIEWS

Book reviews versus current bibliography

We discuss in this section sources of reviews of recent publications on Latin America. The much more numerous sources of listings of new works (many of which may have brief
annotations) are discussed under 'BOOKS & PAMPHLETS'
(in the paragraph 'New publications').

Bibliography of reviews

We know only of one work concerned exclusively with indexing book reviews in the Latin American field. This is the
Guía a las reseñas de libros de y sobre Hispanoamérica
compiled by Antonio Matos. The first issue, published by the
University of Puerto Rico in 1965, covered 1960-1964. It is
now published annually by Ethridge of Detroit, but the years
1966-1971 have not yet come out (although the author hopes
to produce them eventually). As the work began as a single
publication before becoming a periodical, you may well find
it in your library's catalogue under 'Matos' as editor rather
than under its title. It is also sometimes known by its English title, A guide to reviews of books from and about Hispanic America.

A book of reviews

Spring 1973 saw the publication in London of the Latin America review of books, 1, edited by Colin Harding and C.
Roper. No further volume has appeared but since it was intended to be a periodical, you will probably find it catalogued
under its title.

Reviews in periodicals

Since any serious journal in the field will carry its quota of
reviews (albeit often too late in appearance to be much use),
a list is superfluous. If you want to make one, we suggest
you start with the "Lista de publicaciones periódicas

Reviews in periodicals   (cont'd.)

usadas" in Matos's Guía a las reseñas just mentioned. We shall however draw your attention to two titles:

> The Library Journal.   (New York, Bowker, twice monthly since 1876) - gives prompt and informative reviews, directed at American librarians of all important books published in America, which means virtually all important books published in English, arranged by broad subjects. Although it covers all subjects, it is a simple matter to turn to your own speciality and see what is mentioned of Latin American interest;

> The Times Literary Supplement.   (London, Times Newspapers, weekly since 1902) - besides its regular reviewing (by no means restricted to English-language works), it has a special Latin American issue once a year (reviewing books from the region, and books about it from elsewhere).

[LH]

BOOKS & PAMPHLETS

When is a book not a book?

When it is a pamphlet! This is a word variously defined (on a basis of size, binding or price). For UNESCO it is anything with less than a hundred pages, but for most librarians it is simply anything too flimsy to stand upright on a shelf. What matters to the library user is that pamphlets are usually stored separately from books (often in boxes) and that different regulations may govern their use (e.g. borrowing may be forbidden). How you recognise a pamphlet in the catalogue varies from library to library; often there will be a special type of call number or location symbol such as a small 'p' in front of the class mark, but check this with the library staff.

Another distinction apt to be blurred at the edges is that between 'books' meaning single works, and 'serials' meaning anything issued as part of an on-going series. Serials intended to appear at regular intervals are termed 'PERIODI-CALS' (q.v.), but so-called 'irregular serials' will be found sometimes treated as books and sometimes as periodicals.

The all-important author

The scrolls in an ancient Roman library had to be referred to by author, simply because they often had no proper titles: saying that Caesar's work was 'de bello gallico' merely described it, it did not entitle it. Two thousand years on and former necessity now reigns as hallowed tradition. Some of the resulting complexities we discuss under 'CATALOGUES & INDEXES'.

But I only know the title!

Hints on coping with this problem are also given in the section 'CATALOGUES & INDEXES'.

Books & pamphlets

Finding books on particular subjects

This is discussed under 'SUBJECT BIBLIOGRAPHY'.

Learning about new books

Most worthwhile titles in the field, wherever published, are
eventually listed (with brief annotations) in the Handbook of
Latin American studies (see the last paragraph under
'BIBLIOGRAPHIES - GENERAL'), - but this now appears in
two sections, "Humanities" and "Social sciences" each of
which comes out only every other year. Earlier notices may
be found in many of the serious journals of Latin American
studies, but none provides a regular listing that is either
systematic, comprehensive or even consistently prompt.
Apart from these sources, it is necessary to consider new
publications separately by language:-

New books in English

The British bulletin of publications on Latin America, the
West Indies, Portugal and Spain (London, Hispanic & Luso-
Brazilian Council) is a six-monthly selective bibliography.
For more comprehensive coverage of British (and Irish)
books it is necessary to use the British national bibliography (London, British Library Bibliographic Services
Division, weekly with monthly, 4-monthly and annual etc.
cumulations), described in the section 'PRINTED CATA-
LOGUES' (third paragraph). More current are the weekly
lists and publishers' announcements of new U.K. books in
the Bookseller, but these are of limited use for a subject
approach.

Many American books have simultaneous publication in this
country, or appear sooner or later in British editions, and
so are recorded in the B.N.B., the Bookseller, and often in
the British bulletin of publications ... For the others you
can consult the monthly American book publishing record
(New York, Bowker) arranged by the Dewey Decimal

New books in English (cont'd.)

Classification, or the same publisher's Library Journal
(discussed under 'BOOK REVIEWS'). There is also the H.W.
Wilson Company's Cumulative book list (monthly with quarterly and annual cumulations), which attempts to list new publications of the entire English-speaking world, in dictionary
catalogue order.

Books from the West Indies in all languages are listed in the
quarterly Caribbean studies of the University of Puerto Rico
and in the Current Caribbean bibliography (Hato Rey, Biblioteca regional del Caribe y Norte-Sur, monthly with annual
cumulations).

New books in Spanish

There is no really comprehensive guide to new books from
Latin America. An account of the publishing background
which will explain the underlying reasons for many of the
problems you will meet in Latin American bibliography is:

> Naylor, Bernard: "A comprehensive loan collection
> of Latin American material", in Ligue des biblio-
> thèques européennes de recherche: Acquisitions
> from the Third World, papers of the LIBER semi-
> nar 17-19 September 1973, edited by Derek A.
> Clarke. (London, Mansell, 1975, pp.125-143,
> especially pp.133-137).

The best list we have is the monthly Fichero bibliográfico
hispanoamericano (Buenos Aires, Turner); despite its title
this includes books published in Spain, whose output is very
important for Latin America. The Fichero tends to be weak
on official and academic publishing, but can be supplemented
by the Boletín bibliográfico CERLAL (Bogotá, Centro regional de UNESCO para el fomento del libro en América latina -
also monthly). There are also many book dealers who issue
regular lists of new publications from Spanish America (see:

New books in Spanish   (cont'd.)

'BOOKSELLERS'). See also the section 'NATIONAL BIB-
LIOGRAPHY'.

New books in Portuguese

The Fundação Calouste Gulbenkian of Lisbon issues a quarterly Boletim internacional de bibliografia luso-brasileira
but its Brazilian coverage leaves much to be desired. The
Boletim bibliográfico da Biblioteca nacional of Rio constitutes the present Brazilian national bibliography but is neither complete nor up-to-date. Far better for new books are
the monthly Accessions list Brazil issued by the Library of
Congress Office in Rio, and various booksellers' lists, notably Livros novos (São Paulo, Heydecker, also monthly).

New books in other languages

See 'BIBLIOGRAPHIES - MATERIAL IN OTHER LAN-
GUAGES'.

Where to buy books

See the section 'BOOKSELLERS'.

And how to borrow them

See: 'LIBRARY FACILITIES', 'LIBRARY FACILITIES
ABROAD' and 'INTER-LIBRARY LENDING'.

[LH]

BOOKSELLERS

Books in English

Your local bookshop should be able to obtain for you any cur-. rently published book originating in this country or North America even if it carries nothing in stock.

If it proves unsatisfactory, you might care to try:

Blackwells, Broad Street, Oxford.

Alternatively, it is possible to order American publications direct from that country, through such dealers as:

John Coutts Library Service Inc.,
736-738 Cayuga Street,
Lewiston, NY 14092;

Parnassus Book Service,
PO Box 33,
Yarmouth, Mass. 02675;

Yankee Book Peddler Inc.,
PO Box 366,
Fountain Square,
Contoocook, New Hampshire 032229.

Locally published books from the Commonwealth Caribbean may prove difficult to obtain. Our suggestion is:

New Beacon Books Ltd.,
95 Hornsey Lane,
London N.6.

Books in Spanish and Portuguese

Two of the best known booksellers in this country speciali-sing in new Latin American books are:

The Dolphin Book Co. (Tredwr) Ltd.,
Tredwr,
Llangranog, Dyfed, Wales SA44 6B4;

Books in Spanish & Portuguese (cont'd.)

>Grant & Cutler, Ltd.,
>11, Buckingham Street, London WC2N 6BQ.

Both firms issue regular catalogues and carry extensive stock, and are also good sources for English-language material.

Other firms importing books from the region include:

>América Latina (Michexe International Ltd.),
>3rd floor, 71 Fleet Street, London EC4Y 1EU;

>CARILA (Committee against repression in Latin
>29 Islington Park Street, London N1 1QB [America),
>- newspapers, periodicals, new and second hand books;

>Richard S. Gothard (South America) Ltd.,
>Gothard House, Queen Street, Henley-on-Thames,
>Oxfordshire RG9 2AJ;

>Silco Books,
>5 Russell Gardens, London NW11;

>Third World Publications,
>128 Stratford Road, Birmingham B11 1AG.

Customers should appreciate that it is good business practice for firms to list some Latin American items in their catalogues when they do not have them in stock, and they should not criticize them for failing to carry the entire book production of the region!

The following firm is no longer trading at the address given, and enquiries about COLA publications for which they are given as distributors elsewhere in this Guide may be made of the COLA secretary, Mr. G. H. Green at Canning House, 2 Belgrave Square, London SW1X 8PJ:-

>Latin America Books (Maximus Books),
>10b Low Ousegate,
>York.

Booksellers

Booksellers in Latin America and the Caribbean

Exporting and importing books in single-copy lots from Latin
America is a slow, cumbersome and expensive business, beset by difficult and often absurd customs and currency regulations. Naturally, books purchased through a U.K. dealer
will cost more than those ordered direct from the region,
since the British dealer will himself have taken care of the
problems of shipping, customs clearance, currency conversion etc.

You are not however going to find the savings possible by
dealing direct with a Latin American bookseller worth all
the extra bother entailed unless you are able to place substantial, or at least regularly continuing, orders. If you do
try it, then please comply to the letter with your dealer's in-
structions about payment (evading currency control may be
the only way he can stay in business), do not keep him waiting for his money (working capital in the booktrade is always short, particularly under South America's inflationary
conditions), nor begrudge him what may seem to you an un-
usually high percentage mark up over the original published
price. Booksellers willing to cope with all the problems of
supplying books from Latin America are woefully few in
number and need all the help we can give them. And if any
query does arise, write in Spanish (or Portuguese).

If you do decide to try purchasing by mail direct from Latin
America, your best course is probably to discuss the matter
with an experienced librarian in your university library's
book order department. Failing that, you might care to
select from the following list, which has been deliberately
limited to one firm per major country, to keep its length
within reasonable bounds. All those on the list have proved
to be efficient in handling orders for new books, and, in
some cases, also for tracing older material; most issue
regular book lists. There are many other firms equally good
and for several countries it has been almost a matter of
chance which we finally decided to list.

Booksellers

Booksellers in Latin America and the Caribbean

Argentina: Fernando García Cambeiro,
Avenida de Mayo 560,
Buenos Aires;

Bolivia: Editorial Inca,
Bibliografía Boliviana,
Casilla 1514,
Cochabamba;

Brazil: Susan Bach,
Rua Cose Velho 800, Larangeiras,
Rio de Janeiro, RJ;

Chile: Herta Berenguer L.,
Avenida Pocuro 2738,
Casilla 68, Correo 12,
Santiago de Chile;

Colombia: Libros de Colombia,
Apartado aereo 12053;
Calle 22F, no.42C-37,
Bogotá, D. E.

Ecuador: Libri Mundi,
Casilla 3029,
Quito;

Jamaica: Bolivar Bookshop and Gallery,
1d Grove Road,
PO Box 413,
Kingston, 10;

Mexico: M.A.C.H.,
Apartado Postal 7-854,
Mexico 7, D.F.

Peru: E.Iturriaga y Cia, S.A.,
Jirón Ica no.441,
Oficinas 202-204,
Casilla de correos 4640,
Lima;

Booksellers in Latin America and the Caribbean (cont'd.)

Uruguay: Librería Delta,
           Casilla de correos 847,
           Montevideo;

Venezuela: Soberbia S.A.,
            Avenida de Industria, no.4,
            Puente Anauco,
            Caracas.

European booksellers

If material is required from continental Europe, a suitable supplier will probably be found from:

Steele, Colin R., and Walker G.P.M., eds.:
European acquisitions and their bibliographical
control. (Lancaster, Lancaster University
Library, 1975).

Periodicals

Periodicals (i.e. journals, magazines, newspapers) are best ordered direct from their publishers, rather than through a bookseller or other intermediary, and you are strongly advised to consider only airmail subscriptions. When something comes seamail, it is virtually impossible to get missing numbers replaced: by the time you realize something has gone astray and made a claim it will have already become out of print and unobtainable. There is also the point that many publishers' wrappings are too flimsy to stand up to the repeated handling involved in surface mail.

If you do prefer to buy through an agent, most of the above-mentioned dealers will arrange periodical subscriptions (at least for their regular book-buying customers). You can also consult:

Periodicals (cont'd.)

> American Library Association. Joint committee
> to revise List of international subscription
> agents: International subscription agents, an
> international directory, 2.ed.   (Chicago, the
> Association, 1969).

ISBN and ISSN

An increasing number of countries participate in a system of international standard book numbers designed primarily for the computerisation of book ordering. These numbers refer to specific editions (e.g. the paperback and hard cover versions of the same text will have distinct ISBN's). You will facilitate your book ordering if you quote these to your bookseller in addition to the normal information of author, title, publisher and date. So far, ISBN's have come into use in the U.K., North America, Spain and some other European countries, but several Latin American countries have expressed interest and will doubtless adopt the scheme eventually. There is a corresponding ISSN (International standard serial number) for periodicals; it is even possible for a work issued in a monograph series to have both.

Prices

Prices differ considerably from one supplier to another, and there are occasions when individual dealers seem way out of line for a particular item. Generally speaking however, it is a fair rule that (as with most things in life) 'you get what you pay for'. The more expensive firms almost always provide frequent and detailed booklists, a rapid turn-round on orders, sympathetic treatment of claims and general all round efficiency, advantages which fully compensate for their higher mark-up.

Prices (cont'd.)

Remember when comparing prices that most overseas sup-
pliers will add freight and insurance costs to the quoted
price, often as a fixed percentage. A dealer's choice of
currency conversion rates can also materially affect the
cost of doing business with him.

[CRS]

BRITISH UNION CATALOGUE OF
LATIN AMERICANA

What it is

London University's Institute of Latin American Studies has
a special national role as the country's central documentation centre in the field, collecting, compiling and publishing
information on Latin American studies in all British universities.

These activities include the maintenance of a national union
catalogue of Latin-Americana, begun in 1967, which is a
central record in card form of books, pamphlets and periodical titles held in libraries throughout the United Kingdom.
At first contributions came only from libraries within the
University of London, but soon all the "Parry centre" libraries joined, and the scheme was then rapidly expanded
until now there are nearly seventy libraries participating:
university, polytechnic, national, special, embassy etc. These
libraries send in details of their current Latin American and
West Indian acquisitions (including works about the area
published elsewhere), which are then incorporated into the
main file. Older holdings of the contributing libraries are
also being checked and gradually added to the file as staff
time permits.

Arrangement and coverage

The cards in the catalogue are in one alphabetic sequence -
under authors for monographs and under titles for periodicals. Libraries holding a copy of any item are indicated on
its card by a standard symbol (that used in the British union
catalogue of periodicals) called a location. At present the
catalogue registers some 200,000 locations of about 120,000
items.

The catalogue also contains a number of cards from the
Library of Congress in Washington which have no location
noted on them, but provide proof that the items in question
exist even if no British library is yet known to possess a
copy.

British union catalogue of Latin Americana

Publication

At present a selected listing of some 5,000 new items a year
is published as New Latin American titles, circulated to
every contributing library. This list (unlike the card catalogue) is arranged by broad subject headings (sub-arranged
by country), and periodic author indexes are also issued. It
is contemplated that this will shortly be replaced by a series
of subject bibliographies. Both New Latin American titles
and the planned bibliographies include locations.

Consultation

The Institute welcomes enquiries concerning the Union
Catalogue and New Latin American titles, by mail (mailing
address: 31 Tavistock Square, London WC1H 9HA), by telephone (01-387-4055) or in person (to no.35 Tavistock Square;
nearest Underground: Russell Square or Euston Square).

To help visitors make full use of the catalogue the Institute
has a small library of bibliographies, reference works and
guides on Latin America.

[BMH]

CATALOGUES AND INDEXES
HOW TO USE THEM

As simple as ABC?

Alphabetical order is so pervasive in research tools - from
library catalogues to telephone directories - that it is sur-
prising how unaware students often are of its possible pit-
falls. The following notes endeavour to point out some of
these, and also give some help relating to the forms of
names and other headings used in cataloguing. (If you came
to this section looking for information on what library catalogues exist, please turn to 'PRINTED CATALOGUES'; information on indexes to periodicals is provided under
'PERIODICALS').

Alphabetisation

This comes in two varieties, according to the value given to
blank spaces between words. Ignore them and 'New York'
will file after 'Newark'; count them as coming before 'A'
(as most cataloguers and indexes and almost all computerised filing systems do) and 'New York' will come first. The
decision particularly affects the order of Spanish American
compound surnames, e.g. whether 'Echeverri Ortiz, Sancho'
will come before or after all the 'Echeverría' entries. When
you fail to find something, always check that you have not
mistaken the type of alphabetical order used.

Those new to Spanish should remember that Hispanic (but
not Portuguese) practice treats 'Ñ' and the digraphs 'CH'
and 'LL' as separate letters (following 'N', 'C' and 'L'
respectively). Thus a South American gazetteer would have
'Cuzco' before 'Chaco' and 'Antigua' before 'Añatuya'.

Abbreviations usually file as if spelled out: 'McIntosh' as
'Macintosh', 'St. Louis' as 'Saint Louis'.

Catalogues and indexes: how to use them

Personal authorship

Hunting for a book under its author can become irksome
when the catalogue is a large one and the name a common
one, especially if you do not know the forename (or know
only the initial). In such cases you may sometimes save
time by identifying the author and getting his full name first
from a biographical dictionary or directory (e.g. the Library of Congress's National directory of Latin Americanists) - see: 'BIOGRAPHICAL INFORMATION'.

The special problems of Spanish American and Brazilian
name forms are discussed below, followed by remarks on
the complications of corporate and multiple authorship.

Personal names of Spaniards and Spanish Americans

A Spanish speaker will have (at least) two surnames. A
married woman will have her father's surname, followed by
'de' and her husband's surname - e.g. (in library catalogue
form): Contreras de Darío, Rafaela. Anyone else (i.e. a
male or an unmarried female) will use the father's surname
followed by the mother's - with or (usually) without a connecting 'y': Menéndez (y) Pelayo, Marcelino.

Often the second name is dropped in normal usage: e.g.
Castro [Ruz], Fidel, or Ocampo [de Estrada], Victoria.
Sometimes however it is the father's name that is dropped:
[García] Lorca, Federico; this happens particularly often
with Argentine wives: [Duarte de] Perón, Eva. Library catalogues may or may not persist with the full legal form in
such cases.

A confusing South American habit, particularly in Colombia,
is to print the name in full, but to ignore the second element
in determining alphabetical order. The copulas 'de' and 'y'
may likewise be printed but ignored in alphabetising.

Be on your guard against incompetent cataloguers mistaking
a second forename for the main surname, and so perpetra-
ting howlers such as 'Livio Caldas, Tito'.

Catalogues and indexes: how to use them

Personal names of Brazilians and Portuguese

Present practice (which did not become general till the late 1950's) is to file under the last element of the name not a soubriquet: Silva, Arthur da Costa e; Lobato, José Bento Monteiro; but Castelo Branco, Humberto (because 'white castle' is logically a single element).

The soubriquets of relationship (Filho, Junior, Net(t)o, Sobrinho) were until recently ignored, except in the very rare cases where they had become genuine surnames. Nowadays they are generally added to the heading: e.g. Café Filho, João; Coelho Netto, Henrique.

An older custom, which you will still meet in many catalogues and indexes, was to attempt to discover and conform to the author's personal preference: e.g. Machado de Assis, Joaquim Maria (even though 'Machado' was his mother's name).

A still older custom was to arrange by first name, so that 'Gregório de Matos' for instance, would file under 'G'. This was the normal procedure in Brazil until about the middle of last century; even today any list of names drawn up by a Brazilian who is not a professional indexer or librarian will probably be so arranged. This applies even to some provincial telephone directories. Given the social importance of Christian names in Brazil it is actually a very practical arrangement.

Unfortunately, whichever of these three orders is used, two further complications remain. Firstly comes the choice between actual usage (which may well be inconsistent) and the full legal name. So be prepared to look for Lins do Rêgo under 'Cavalcanti' and for Kubitschek under 'Oliveira'. Library catalogues nowadays generally accept the short everyday form, but still tend to jib at names lacking any surname (e.g. Washington Luis) or any forename (e.g. Barbosa Lima Sobrinho): these will almost always be expanded, however unhelpful that may be. Names consisting of one Christian name and a soubriquet (e.g. Adonias Filho) may have to

Personal names of Brazilians and Portuguese (cont'd.)

be searched for under the unused surname (in this case,
'Aguiar') or may even be filed under the soubriquet.
National heroes universally known by nicknames (Pele,
Tiradentes, Aleijadinho) may be under their surnames (i.e.
Nascimento, Silva, Lisboa ...). Of course there should be
referenced from the form you expect to the one the library
has chosen, but do not count on it.

The other complication is spelling. Orthographic reform has
been going on in Portuguese almost continually since 1910,
but individuals (and their publishers) have different ideas on
how far it should apply to personal names ... and no one
seems consistent. So always try both 'Beça' and 'Bessa',
'Correa' and 'Correia', 'Guimaraens' and 'Guimarães',
'Lafaiete' and 'Lafayette', 'Mello' and 'Melo', 'Moraes' and
'Morais', 'Penna' and 'Pena', 'Queirós' and 'Queiroz' etc.
etc. Brazilian libraries and reference works tend to prefer
the modernised spelling; British and American library catalogues seem to persist with whichever form was used in the
author's first book that that particular library happened to
acquire.

Prefixes

Iberian surnames abound in prefixes: 'de', 'del', 'de la(s)',
'de los' in Spanish, and 'de', 'da(s)', 'do(s)' in Portuguese.
These are ignored in filing when they occur at the beginning
of the surname (as long as they are written separately).
Spanish speakers also ignore them for the purpose of alphabetical order even when they come in the middle of a name.

A Hispanic woman's married name can even have two prefixes together, as Amelia Agostini de del Río, wife of Ángel
del Río.

Catalogues and indexes: how to use them

Multiple authorship

Works written in collaboration ('joint authorship') are indexed under the author first named on the title-page, so it is
better to know his name in full rather than the bare surnames
of both (or all) the writers involved.

A work made up of clearly differentiated contributions by
several writers (whether they planned it so themselves or
not) constitutes 'multiple authorship'. Such works are usually under the editor, except for conference papers which
usually go under the name of the conference (but see the
section 'CONFERENCES & SOCIETIES'). There is however
an increasing tendency to put all works of multiple authorship under their titles.

This guide (which tries to follow the decisions of the United
States National Union Catalog in all references) shows just
how much inconsistency exists in current practice.

Institutions and societies

A corporate body is often treated as an author for anything
issued in its name or by its authority, and usually appears
in the catalogue under its full official name. (Note that some
libraries will always use the English form of this if one exists but others insist on the original language title). See
'ABBREVIATIONS & ACRONYMS' for help if you do not
know the full form of any name.

Earlier practice (still very much in evidence in library
catalogues) made a distinction between societies (under
their names) and institutions, defined as physical entities
with a fixed abode, which were catalogued under 'place' -
e.g. Bogotá. Inter-American housing and planning center;
Rio de Janeiro. Academia brasileira de letras.

Sometimes the difference between the new practice and the
old one is just a matter of punctuation: e.g. 'New York Public Library' versus 'New York. Public library' - but even
punctuation makes a big difference in filing position in a

Catalogues and indexes: how to use them

Institutions and societies (cont'd.)

large catalogue. 'Place', too, is a vague concept; an old-style catalogue entry for, say, the University of Essex could equally well be under 'Essex', 'Colchester' or 'Wivenhoe'.

And whether a library catalogues institutions under title or place, there is still the possibility that it may regard public funded bodies as branches of government (which go under the name of the country, province or other unit of administration). Thus, for example, you might find 'Brazil. Instituto nacional do livro' or 'Colombia. Instituto Caro y Cuervo'.

Official authorship

Author headings for officially sponsored or published material present several problems which we discuss in the sections on 'OFFICIAL PUBLICATIONS' and on 'LAW & LEGISLATION'.

But I only know the title!

Knowing only the title of a work is probably the commonest source of frustration in using a library catalogue; few libraries provide more than 'author' and 'subject' catalogues. 'Author' catalogues do however almost always include some title entries - for anonymous works, often for works of multiple authorship, and sometimes for works with especially distinctive titles. Title entries are also made for periodicals, although these may be in a separate catalogue; see the section on 'PERIODICALS'.

When title entries are made, some traditional libraries prefer to file them under the first significant word (variously defined), but usual practice is 'under the first word not an article'. This rule may be unintentionally breached from ignorance, e.g. the Portuguese article 'a' may be mistaken for a preposition (and vice versa). Even a filer who knows the language may be confused by titles beginning 'O que ...' (where 'o' is grammatically a pronoun).

Catalogues and indexes: how to use them

Tracing the author from title bibliographies

When you only know the title and have looked for it in vain
in the catalogue, you may, with much patience and some
luck, track it down (and so find the all-important author)
through various published bibliographies. Where to look
depends on the language of the book and on when and where
it was published.

British books in print, compiled each January, includes title
entries for anything currently available in this country. The
U.S. equivalent, Books in print, has a separate title section
(in two volumes) for books and pamphlets on sale there each
July. The corresponding work for Spain and Spanish America, Libros en venta, comes out every ten years, with annual
supplements: each part is in a single volume with a 'títulos'
section at the back. For current Brazilian imprints there
are only the individual publishers' catalogues - these are
unlikely to be generally available in your library but you
may be allowed to see them if you make special enquiry of
its book-ordering department.

Title indexes for works too recent to be included in the
above can be found in the Bookseller (weekly) and British
national bibliography (weekly with monthly and quarterly
cumulations): the Bookseller also includes periodic indexes
to books programmed for publication later in the year. Less
prompt, but aiming to cover English language publications
throughout the world is the Cumulative book index (monthly
with quarterly and annual cumulations). For Spanish language publications there is a title index in each month's
Fichero bibliográfico hispanoamericano.

Tracing an out-of-print book by its title may be done (i) by
computer searching of machine-readable catalogues: see
the section on 'DATA BANKS'; (ii) by consulting some of
the works listed in our section 'PRINTED CATALOGUES',
or (iii) by laboriously checking through the cumulation volumes of the British national bibliography (back to 1950),
the Cumulative book index (back to 1928) and similar works,

Catalogues and indexes: how to use them

Tracing the author from title bibliographies (cont'd.)

or through the monthly issues of Fichero bibliográfico hispanoamericano, or through the indexes to the various national bibliographies, such as the defunct Bibliografia brasileira (1938-1966) - see the section 'NATIONAL BIBLIOGRAPHY'.

If all else fails it may be possible, if the book's subject is precisely known, to locate it using the subject catalogue:

Subject catalogues

Most British libraries have separate 'Author' and 'Subject' catalogues, although works about a person or institution or organisation are often filed in the 'Author' catalogue (along with any works by them), and this is then, strictly speaking, a 'Name' catalogue. Such an arrangement is quite illogical, but happens to be convenient for the cataloguers.

The 'Subject' catalogue proper may be arranged in alphabetic or classified order. The latter is more usual in Britain and can have several advantages - if you are prepared to give the system a little study (ask the library staff to explain). Since the classified catalogue needs an alphabetical key (usually called the 'Subject index' or 'Subject guide'), there is a natural temptation to go directly from the latter to the shelves, overlooking the fact that the classified catalogue will always differ in many ways from the actual shelf arrange- ment (e.g. regarding books on several subjects, or material whose format precludes its presence on the normal shelving).

The alphabetical subject catalogue is an American idea; this frequently leads those British libraries that have adopted it to follow American practice in the choice of headings - not just 'corn' to mean 'maize' or 'corporation' in the sense of 'limited liability company', but 'rapid transit' instead of 'urban public transport', 'eminent domain' for 'compulsory purchase' and 'aeronautics, commercial' for 'civil aviation'.

Catalogues and indexes: how to use them

Subject catalogues (cont'd.)

Most North American (and a few British) libraries actually
integrate their alphabetical subject and author catalogues into one sequence, which is then known as a 'dictionary catalogue'. This may seem convenient, but it produces its own
problems: it may not be, for instance, clear why official
publications of 'Washington (state)' precede works about
'Washington D.C.' - and why both come before 'Washington
County (Arkansas)' but after 'Washington, George' (whether
as author or as subject). Similar problems will present
themselves with such headings as 'Mexico', 'Panama', 'São
Paulo', 'Buenos Aires'...

The commonest mistake in using an alphabetical subject
catalogue or index (including the index to a classified catalogue) is to choose too broad a heading; e.g. readers wanting
something on coffee in São Paulo tend to look under 'Agriculture - Brazil' rather than under 'São Paulo - coffee
industry' or 'Coffee industry - São Paulo' (which way round
differs from one library or index to another, and even from
one subject to another). Always look under the most specific
subject first, and then - if you draw a blank - gradually
widen the search, never vice-versa.

[LH]

CENSUSES

When they start

Spanish American official censuses go back a surprisingly long way - to 1579 in fact, but few early censuses were ever published and such as still survive in manuscript are not always in the appropriate national archives. The 1579-82 Mexican census, for instance, has been acquired by the University of Texas, whilst the 1700 census of Lima is in the Biblioteca nacional of Madrid and the Foreign and Commonwealth Office holds the first reliable British colonial census, that of Port of Spain in 1835. The Oxford University School of Geography and Syracuse University have recently set up a joint project to collect and collate material surviving from the Spanish imperial censuses of 1776 to 1800.

Latin American printed censuses begin with those of Chile (1777), Honduras (1791) and Mexico (1793). There is a printed census for El Salvador in 1807; Colombia (which then included Ecuador, Panama and Venezuela) begins in 1835, Cuba in 1827. The first general census of the British West Indies was taken in 1843 and there were other mid-nineteenth-century printed censuses for Bolivia and Uruguay. Argentina began in 1869, Brazil in 1872, and Guatemala, Paraguay, Peru and Puerto Rico had all taken censuses before the end of the century. The Dominican Republic had its first census only in 1920, and Haiti and Surinam did not start until 1950.

Several individual provinces, towns and colonies have their own local censuses available for dates much earlier than these.

Frequency

Most countries take their national census decennially, usually in the 'zero' year of the decade, although, until World War II, most British colonial administrations held them in the same year as the U.K. domestic census. Wars, revolutions and other causes have interrupted the sequence from time to time. Thus Brazil had no census in 1910 or 1930; Peru took none between 1876 and 1940; a cholera epidemic frustrated

Censuses

Frequency (cont'd.)

Jamaica's 1851 census, and economic stringency prevented several British colonies from holding their 1931 censuses.

The United Nations made an effort, not wholly successful, to get all countries in the region to hold a census in 1960. This persuaded several countries to join those with 'zero' year censuses.

Bibliography

Limited to demographic censuses (except in so far as certain countries - e.g. Brazil - issue all types of census data in one publication), but otherwise comprehensive is:

> University of Texas at Austin. Population research center: International population census bibliography. Census bibliography no.1: Latin America and the Caribbean. (Austin, Bureau of Business Research, 1965, and supplement, 1968).

Including economic censuses, but omitting anything not held in any Paris library is:

> Université de Paris. Institut des hautes études de l'Amérique latine. Centre de documentation: Bibliographie des recensements démographiques et économiques des pays d'Amérique latine existants à Paris. (Paris, Centre de documentation de l'Institut, 1967).

Censuses of industry and services are also listed in the "Americas" section (pp.35-68) of:

> United Nations. Statistical office: Bibliography of industrial and distributive-trade statistics, 4.ed. (New York, UNO, 1975).

Censuses

Bibliography (cont'd.)

For population censuses of the Commonwealth there is:

Kuczynski, Robert R.: Demographic survey of
the British colonial empire. Volume 3: West
Indian and American territories. (London,
Oxford University Press, 1953).

Population data for Mexico is covered in essay form by:

Cook, Sherburne F., and Borah, W.W.: "Materials
for the demographic history of Mexico 1500-1960",
in their: Essays in population history, Mexico and
the Caribbean. (Berkeley, University of California Press, 1971, vol. 1, pp.2-72).

Locating censuses in the library

Census material is entered in most library catalogues under
the name of the appropriate government department (usually
as a sub-heading under the name of the country or other political unit). Unfortunately the hierarchy of departments may
produce complications. Thus the Brazilian census of 1940
was issued by the Comissão censitário nacional of the
Serviço nacional de recenseamento of the Conselho nacional
de estatística, itself a branch of the Instituto brasileiro de
geografia e estatística - and may have been recorded in the
library catalogue under any one or a combination of these
headings. ... And the administrative set-up was different
for earlier and later censuses. In the West Indies there is
the complication that some censuses were undertaken by individual territories whilst others were co-operative projects.
The 1946 West Indian census was published in Kingston by
the Jamaican Central Bureau of Statistics; the 1960 census
was divided into the West Indian population census covering
the Westerly and Northerly territories, issued in Jamaica,
and the Eastern Caribbean population census (Guiana, Trinidad and Tobago, Barbados and the Windwards) published by
the Central statistical office of Trinidad and Tobago.

Censuses

Locating censuses in the library (cont'd.)

Should you have difficulty, try the sub-heading 'Census'
under the name of the country, in either the 'author' or 'subject' catalogues - or ask the library staff.

Censuses elsewhere

It is seldom practicable to obtain census material through
interlibrary loan, except where summaries or census data
on special topics have been separately published. The bulk
of the material usually makes it cheaper for the researcher
to visit another library that possesses the desired item, than
to have it sent for him. Nor can libraries usually spare staff
time to undertake the extraction of data for researchers unable to make a personal visit.

International agreements between governments to exchange
official publications are supposed to ensure the availability
of all recent foreign censuses at the Department of Industry's Statistics and Market Intelligence Library. After fif-
teen years they are then intended to be transferred to the
Official Publications Library of the British Library Reference Division (the old British Museum State Paper Room) to
fill any possible gaps in the BLRD's collection.

Unfortunately the exchange scheme does not function perfectly. Also, much material at the British Library is stored
at the Woolwich Depository (and may not have been added
yet to the General Catalogue); it is however made available
on request, even if a special search has to be made, and
most of it is included in the special catalogue of official publications. Foreign census material is also collected by the
Office of Population Censuses and Surveys.

SCONUL Latin American Group is preparing a union list of
British and Irish library holdings of all Latin American and
West Indian censuses. From preliminary returns for this
list, it would seem that there is little material in the country
earlier than about 1890, and no extensive holdings before

Censuses elsewhere (cont'd.)

about 1950. There is also a generally greater availability of
material from some countries (e.g. Brazil) than from
others (e.g. Mexico).

Alternative sources of census information

Although published censuses are necessarily selective in the
data included, they are still much more detailed than is
necessary for many purposes. Where a particular census is
not available, or where the full census is not needed, a good
substitute is often provided by such publications as the
Anuarios estadísticos of the various countries. There may
also exist an official survey or sample census. See the section 'STATISTICS'.

[LH]

CONFERENCES & MEETINGS

Announcements

News of forthcoming conferences on Latin American topics is given in the "Professional notes" section of the American Hispanic American historical review (quarterly since 1918), in the Informationsdienst of the Arbeitsgemeinschaft Deutsche Lateinamerika-Forschung (quarterly since 1966) and in Latinskaia Amerika of the Institut Latinskoi Ameriki of the Academy of Sciences of the USSR (bimonthly since 1969). The Latin American Research Review also has a regular listing, limited to meetings in North America.

Besides these, there are the more general sources of news about forthcoming meetings such as Forthcoming international scientific and technical conferences (London, ASLIB, quarterly) and the Annual international congress calendar (Brussels, Union of international associations, since 1961).

Published proceedings

Published conference papers can usually be found in library catalogues under the official name of the conference, but it is sometimes difficult to discover precisely what this is. Some library catalogues try to help by grouping all such papers under one heading (such as 'Conference' or 'International conference'), or by consistently using the English form of the name. When in difficulty, look up under (in turn) the name of the sponsoring organisation, the title of the collected papers (if any), the editor, or the name of any prominent contributor (preferably the one first named on the title-page or the author of the first paper published). The British Library Lending Division has produced since 1964 a regular key-word Index of conference proceedings received (monthly), with annual and decennial cumulations). The decennial cumulation of the Index has the title BLL Conference Index. The work indexes conferences but not individual papers. Conference proceedings acquired by the United States Library of Congress since late 1973 are listed, by 'author' (i.e. name or sponsor of conference), by title (i.e. title of the proceedings as published), by subject, and, (in the 'Area studies'

Conferences & meetings

Published proceedings (cont'd.)

section) under 'Latin America', in G.K. Hall & Co. of Boston's Conference publications guide (monthly, with annual cumulations).

Abstracts of papers presented at conferences of the Society for Latin American Studies appear in special supplements to the Society's Bulletin.

Sponsoring organisations

For names and addresses of the more important sponsors of conferences, see the section 'SOCIETIES & ASSOCIATIONS'.

[LH]

CONTEMPORARY ARCHIVE ON
LATIN AMERICA

What it is

The Contemporary Archive on Latin America is a library, established in July 1976 "to provide a comprehensive source of information on contemporary developments in Latin America and on the relationship of Great Britain to the region". Its collection stresses newspapers and periodical material (over 300 periodicals currently received) particularly in the areas of social, political and economic change, legal, religious and governmental institutions, and patterns of trade, investment and finance. It is located at 1, Cambridge Terrace, Regent's Park, London NW1 4JL; telephone 01-487-5277. The director is Mr. Larry Wright.

N.B. Its acronym, CALA, can also mean "Canadian association of Latin Americanists".

Access

The Archive is an independent private organisation, registered as a charity. It is managed by trustees and is dependent upon membership income. Membership costs a minimum of £5 a year (£2.50 to students and old age pensioners), but occasional use is permitted at 50 pence per day (25p. to students and O.A.P.'s).

The collection is on open access to users. Photocopies of material can be supplied and help given with queries. Opening hours are 10:00 to 17:30 Mondays to Fridays, but access at other times may be possible by prior arrangement.

Publications

CALA issues a quarterly Bulletin of its activities and library acquisitions (often with good bibliographies), irregular Fact sheets on various topics, and a monthly Clipping service (printed or on microfiche) covering eleven UK newspapers and news magazines, plus the daily Le Monde.

[LH]

DATA BANKS & INFORMATION IN
MACHINE READABLE FORMAT

Cumulative indexes

A literature search can be speeded up enormously if the essential bibliographic tools, such as abstracting journals and periodical indexes, are in machine-readable form. Such publication is still largely confined to rather specialised subject fields (e.g. Commonwealth agricultural bureaux abstracts) but there are already a number of important general sources you should be aware of. Dissertation abstracts is one example (see the section 'THESES'); others include Historical abstracts, Sociological abstracts and Social sciences citation index. Current affairs are covered by the New York Times information bank which abstracts articles from sixty-odd journals and newspapers from many countries.

Bibliography

Books and other publications from all over the world can be traced, by author, title or subject, through the MARC (MAchine Readable Catalog) series of data bases: these presently include LC MARC, alias LIBCON (works acquired by the United States Library of Congress from 1968 onwards), UK MARC (works registered in the British national bibliography since it started in January 1950), and Western European accessions to the British library (Reference Division), from 1970. Other national MARC systems are being developed for Spanish America ('MARCAL'), Brazil ('CALCO'), Spain ('IBERMARC'), France, Italy and elsewhere.

Statistics

There are also obvious advantages in having census figures, election returns and other statistics in machine-readable format. Many statistics are no longer published in conventional form at all; one Latin American national statistical agency that has gone over to the computer in a big way is

Statistics (cont'd.)

the Departamento administrativo nacional de estadística (DANE) of Colombia. Developments in this field and in the wider applications of computerisation in Latin America are covered in:

> Barquín, Ramón C.: "Computation in Latin America, an annotated bibliography", Latin American research review, 11(1), Jan. 1976, pp. 75-102.

There are also many American academic institutions and commercial organisations that maintain data archives of interest to the Latin Americanist. The most important is the Latin American Data Bank of the University of Florida, established in 1965, which possesses some 300 data sets: census returns, social surveys, election returns, legislature voting records and (to a lesser extent) economic data; much of the archive is unique, having derived from sources that no longer exist. For a survey of what is available there, and elsewhere in North America, see:

> Data banks and archives for social science research on Latin America. (Gainesville, Consortium of Latin American Studies Programs, 1975);

> Quantitative social science research on Latin America, edited by Robert S. Byars and J.L. Love. (Urbana, University of Illinois Press, 1973).

For Europe, see:

> Tomberg, Alex: Data bases in Europe: a directory to machine-readable data bases and data banks in Europe. (London, ASLIB, 1976).

Historians may like to know that Latin America in basic historical collections, a world-wide 'working guide' by Russell H. Bartley and S. L. Wagner (Stanford, Hoover Institution, 1972) contains a brief note on data banks.

Availability

Few of these services are at the moment available to the
library user in this country, but the field is one of rapid
developments and you should consult a knowledgeable assistant on your own library's staff.

One of the best developed services in the U.K. is that provided by the University of London, whose staff and postgraduate students may already make on-line searches of a
variety of data bases, both British and American. Details
from: Central Information Services, Senate House, Malet
Street, London WC1E 7HU (telephone 01-636-4514, exten-
sion 937).

There is also the national service, 'BLAISE' (British Lib-
rary Automated Information SE-rvice), to which it is hoped
all major libraries in the Kingdom will eventually be linked.
This began in April 1977 with the MEDLARS databases from
the U.S. National Library of Medicine, and included by
October 1977 the UK MARC and the U.S. Library of Con-
gress MARC files. Other data bases, including the British
Library's own databases are being considered for addition.
Searches can be undertaken by post to the MEDLARS unit,
British Library Lending Division, Boston Spa, Wetherby,
West Yorkshire LS23 7BQ, or by personal call to the
Science Reference Library (Bayswater Branch), 10 Por-
chester Gardens, London W2. Further information about
BLAISE from Miss Shirley Nicholson, British Library Bib-
liographic Services Division, 7 Rathbone Street, London W1P
2AL, telephone 01-636-1544.

Cost

Computer time is expensive. Most services will have trained
staff to help you select the data base best suited to your purpose, and to design your search strategy. The cost even so
can be appreciable: that of the average enquiry of the
Florida Data Bank lies between $100 and $150. Most institutions require the user to pay only a part (and often only a

Cost (cont'd.)

nominal part) of the actual cost. The current rate for using the BLAISE postal service, for instance, is of the order of £7 to £10 plus 10 pence per page of print-out, plus V.A.T.

You are strongly advised to check what you are likely to have to pay at the outset!

[LH, EL]

DIRECTORIES

Library provision

No category of reference material is probably more ill-provided in British library collections on Latin America than directories. This is perfectly understandable. The preëminent use of a directory being to supply the current address etc. of an organisation or individual, it is almost pointless for a library to buy any it cannot afford regularly to replace whenever new editions are issued, which usually means every twelvemonth.

For many purposes general international directories such as (in the academic field) The World of learning will provide quite adequate information on Latin America and obviate the need to consult special works on the region.

Even in some of the country's largest Latin American collections you may not find any but the most general directory material, and it is to this that the following notes are largely confined.

Telephone directories

In Latin America, as elsewhere, telephone directories are almost always the quickest and simplest way of finding any current address, which is why we put this category first, even though very few libraries have any. Two libraries within walking distance of each other in the City of London, the City Business Library in Basinghall Street and the Department of Industry's Statistics and Market Intelligence Library on Ludgate Hill both have an extensive range of Latin American telephone directories. In the West End there is the Westminster Central Reference Library (St. Martin's Street, Charing Cross) which has telephone directories of most of the region's major cities.

Directories

General directories covering all Latin America

A useful annual which you might hope to find in any good collection is:

> Anuario de los paises de A. L. A. L. C. (Buenos Aires, Instituto de publicidad y estadística, 1966-) - contains a commercial directory for the ALALC countries, among other things.

Wretchedly printed, but fairly recent and presumably intended to be updated from time to time is:

> Guía C. B. A. de referencia latinoamericana 1973/4, edited by Eduardo Darino. (Montevideo, CBA, 1974) - a guide to cultural institutions and associations, arranged by country, sub-arranged by type of institution: 'Academias', 'alianzas culturales', 'archivos', 'asociaciones' ...

A mine of information, whose lack of a name index makes consultation quite wearisome is:

> Sable, Martin H.: Master directory for Latin America, containing ten directories covering organizations, associations and institutions in the fields of agriculture, business-industry-finance, communications, education-research, government ... [etc. etc.] (Los Angeles, Latin American center of UCLA, 1965).

Brief but more recent:

> Glossary of institutions concerned with Latin America. (Toronto, Canadian Association of Latin Americanists, 1974).

Among more specialised lists are:

> Consejo latinoamericano de ciencias sociales. Secretaría ejecutiva: Directorio de centros latinoamericanos de investigaciones en ciencias sociales. (Buenos Aires, CLACSO, 1968);

Directories

General directories covering all Latin America (cont'd.)

> Hilton, Ronald: The scientific institutions of Latin
> America, with special reference to their organi-
> zation and information facilities. (Stanford, Cali-
> fornia Institute of International Studies, 1970);

> Organisation for economic coöperation and de-
> velopment. Development Centre: Directory of
> development research and training institutes in
> Latin America. (Paris, OECD, 1973);

> Pan American Institute of Geography and History:
> Guía de instituciones que cultivan la historia de
> América. (Mexico City, Instituto panamericano
> de geografía e historia, 1971);

> Bowker editores Argentina S.A.: La empresa del
> libro en América latina, 2.ed. (Buenos Aires,
> Bowker, 1974);

> Stromberg, Ann: Philanthropic foundations in
> Latin America. (New York, Russell Sage
> Foundation, 1968).

See also the section 'SOCIETIES & ASSOCIATIONS'.

Other sources

A variety of guides, handbooks, annuals and other publications may from time to time be found to provide the information one wants. The ever-useful South American handbook
for instance (see section: 'HANDBOOKS AND GUIDES') has
lists of travel agents, hotels, embassies (of all major English speaking countries) and miscellaneous 'useful addresses'. Knowing where one might profitably look comes only
with practice, and this is a field where you should never
hesitate to seek help from the library staff - they may even,
in desperation, have built up their own card file of Latin
American addresses.
[LH]

ENCYCLOPAEDIAS

General encyclopaedias

Whilst any good general encyclopaedia should provide a quick
reference source for basic facts about Latin America, as
about anywhere else, your attention is particularly drawn to
one which (allowing for when it was first published) is about
the most comprehensive encyclopaedia generally available,
besides being specifically intended for Spanish and Spanish-
American users. It is a mine of information on anything
from statistics of the climate of Guayaquil to the (early 20th-
century) uniforms of the Argentine army (illustrated in full-
colour plates):

> Enciclopedia universal ilustrada europeo-americana.
> (Barcelona, Espasa, 70 vols in 72, 1907-30, plus 10
> vol "apéndice", 1930-33 and regular "suplementos",
> currently biennial, thereafter) - unfortunately the
> supplements can hardly remedy the progressive out-
> dating of the main text.

Also useful, particularly for information on their country of
publication, are the various general encyclopaedias from
Latin America. Notable among these are:

> Diccionario enciclopédico UTEHA, 2.ed.   (Mexico
> City, Unión tipográfica editorial hispanoamericana,
> 10 vols, 1964-68, plus 2 vol "apéndice", 1967);

> Enciclopédia Barsa. (Rio de Janeiro, Encyclo-
> paedia britannica do Brasil, 16 vols, 1964) - also
> published in a Spanish version by the Encyclo-
> paedia britannica's Buenos Aires subsidiary;

> Gran Omeba, diccionario enciclopédico ilustrado.
> (Buenos Aires, Omeba, 12 vols, 1965);

> Grande enciclopédia Delta-Larousse. (Rio de
> Janeiro, Delta, 12 vols, 1970) - probably the
> widest Brazilian coverage of all modern
> Brazilian encyclopaedias.

Encyclopaedias

Encyclopaedias of Latin America

Editorial Futuro of Buenos Aires produced a Diccionario enciclopédico de las Américas in 1947, Presses Universitaires de France an Encyclopédie de l'Amérique latine in 1954, and the Sociedad latinoamericana de Japón has produced five editions of its Latin American encyclopaedia (in Japanese) since 1939, the latest in 1968. There is now something in English:

> Encyclopedia of Latin America, edited by Helen Delpar. (New York, McGraw Hill, 1974) - an authoritative work with signed articles by over 100 contributors, but with few maps: most of the illustrations are portraits. Excludes the Commonwealth Caribbean and concentrates on the post-Independence period.

Limiting itself largely but not entirely to history is:

> Martin, Michael R., and Lovett, G.H.: Encyclopedia of Latin-American history, revised ed. by L.R.Hughes. (Indianapolis, Bobbs-Merrill, 1968) - despite its title has articles for men of letters like Neruda, Borges and Gilberto Freyre but not for such political figures as Frondizi or Kubitschek.

An older work of interest (if only because of its size) is:

> Diccionario enciclopédico hispanoamericano de literatura, ciencias, artes. (New York, 23 vols, 1938).

National encyclopaedias

More specialised (and therefore generally more detailed) are the various encyclopaedias devoted to individual countries. Such are:

> Diccionario enciclopédico del Perú, ilustrado, por Alberto Tauro. (Lima, Mejía Baca, 3 vols, 1966-67, and "apendice", 1975);

Encyclopaedias

National encyclopaedias (cont'd.)

Diccionario Porrúa: historia, biografía y geografía de Mexico, 2.ed. (Mexico City, Porrúa, 1965, plus "suplemento", 1966);

Enciclopedia de México. (Mexico City, Instituto de la Enciclopedia, 1966-) - in progress;

Encyclopedie van de Nederlandse Antillen, ed. H. Hoetink. (Amsterdam, Elsevier, 1969);

Encyclopaedie van Nederlandsch West-Indië. (Leiden, Brill, 1914-17);

Gran enciclopedia argentina, por Diego A. de Santillán. (Buenos Aires, Ediar, 8 vols, 1956-63, plus "apéndice", 1964);

Grande enciclopédia portuguêsa e brasileira. Parte complementar: Brasil. (Lisbon, Editorial Enciclopédia, 1967-) - being published in fascicules, very slowly: the last completed volume, the second, issued in 1973, had only reached 'Geise'.

Encyclopaedias and dictionaries of national history, etc.

Rather more limited in their compass are such works as the Scarecrow Press series of Latin American historical dictionaries, edited by Alva Curtis Wilgus. So far published are the volumes for Bolivia, by Dwight B. Heath, The British Caribbean, by William R. Lux, Chile, by Salvatore Bizzaro, Ecuador, by Albert W. Bork and G. Maier, Guatemala, by Richard E. Moore, Nicaragua, by Harvey K. Meyer, Panama, by Basil and Anne Hedrick, Paraguay, by Charles J. Kolinski, Puerto Rico and the U.S. Virgin Islands, by Kenneth R. Farr, El Salvador, by Philip F. Flemion, Uruguay, by Jean L. Willis, and Venezuela, by Donna K. and G. A. Rudolph.

Encyclopaedias

(cont'd.)

To these may be added:

> Diccionario histórico argentino, dirigido por
> Ricardo Piccirilli [y otros]. (Buenos Aires,
> Ediciones históricas argentinas, 6 vols,
> 1953-55);

> Fuentes, Jordi, and Cortes, L. : Diccionario
> histórico de Chile, 2.ed. (Santiago, Pacífico,
> 1965, and later reprints);

> Fuentes, Jordi, and Cortes, L.: Diccionario
> político de Chile, 1810-1966. (Santiago, Orbe,
> 1967);

> Nôvo dicionário de história do Brasil, ilustrado,
> redação de Brasil Bandecchi [e outros]. (São
> Paulo, Melhoramentos, 1970).

Locating and using

As will be seen from the above, a general (but not invari-
able) practice in library catalogues is to list encyclopaedias by their titles. There is also the possibility of entry
under the publisher if he has commissioned the work (e.g.
you may find the Nôvo dicionário de história do Brasil in
some library catalogues under 'Melhoramentos' or 'Edições Melhoramentos'). Note that 'encyclopaedia' loses an
'a' to become 'encyclopedia' in North American usage, and
that 'dic(c)ionario' has two 'c's in Spain and Spanish
America, but only one in Brazil.

A peculiarity of many large encyclopaedias that is easily
overlooked is the existence of the index volume (or volumes);
despite the (normally) alphabetical arrangement of topics,
you should always make your first approach through the index when there is one: it will save you time in the long run.

Encyclopaedias

Handbooks

Another source for general information, particularly when up-to-dateness is important, is the briefer but more regularly and thoroughly revised handbook; such works we discuss in the section 'HANDBOOKS AND GUIDES'.

[EL, PN]

GRANTS, BURSARIES, SCHOLARSHIPS

Reference books

Every other year UNESCO issues its Study abroad, which includes information on sources of financial support. Arrangement is by country of study, subdivided by subject.

The British Council publishes a rather briefer Scholarships abroad, which is annual.

Also intended as annual (although the 1977/79 volume is only the fifth of a series starting with 1969/70) is the Grants register (London, St. James Press) which limits itself to postgraduate awards available to nationals of English-speaking countries (viz. Australia, Canada, Ireland, New Zealand, South Africa, the United Kingdom and the U.S.A.). Arrangement is alphabetical by grant-making body, but the subject index shows whether the award is tenable in particular geographic regions (e.g. 'LA', meaning 'Latin America') and whether it is restricted to citizens of particular countries (e.g. 'UK').

The Directory of grant-making trusts was published in 1968 (5.ed., 1977) by the Charities Aid Fund of the National Council of Social Service, and lists only such trusts as make grants to charitable institutions. Individuals with unusual research projects may, however, find some information in it of occasional use.

Other sources

Universities and other educational bodies often have some funds available which they may not publicise, but which heads of departments will know about. You should also enquire of the D.E.S.

If you hope to do research in a particular country, you may find it useful to contact the cultural attaché at the appropriate embassy or high commission. Some of the larger Latin American countries award regular scholarships to foreign students: the Brazilian Foreign Office (for instance) gives

Other sources (cont'd.)

two six-month scholarships every year in each of a large number of foreign countries, those for the U.K. being awarded through the agency of the British Council.

Latin American research awards

Specifically on awards to postgraduate students and researchers in the Latin American field is the pamphlet:

> Redclift, Michael and Corkill, D.: Postgraduate and research awards available in the field of Latin American studies.   (London, Institute of Latin American Studies, 1972).

[LH]

HANDBOOKS AND GUIDES

General handbooks

The section 'ENCYCLOPAEDIAS' has already covered the
more comprehensive and discursive type of general reference work. Although there is no hard and fast division, handbooks tend to be briefer and more geared to giving rapid
access to basic facts, and usually undergo more regular and
more thorough revision, and so provide much more up-to-
date information. Another difference is that most encyclopaedias arrange their material, dictionary fashion, in alphabetical order, whilst handbooks tend to adopt a more
systematic presentation.

Various international annuals will provide current information on the individual states of the world and on international
and regional organisations. Preëminent are The Statesman's
yearbook (London, Macmillan, 1864-   ) and The International yearbook and statesmen's who's who (London,
Kelly's Directories, 1953-   ). Although primarily political
these also provide much economic, historical, cultural and
other information.

Specialising in Latin America is the South American handbook (annual since 1924, although published earlier as the
Anglo-South American handbook). Despite its title, it has
always included Mexico, Central America and the West
Indies. As the name of the publishers, Trade and Travel
Publications, suggests, it is aimed at the businessman and
tourist (what to buy, what to wear, what to see, how to get
about), but it is also a mine of general and historical information. Certainly you should never visit Latin America
without taking a copy with you.

A German equivalent to the South American handbook, with
rather more statistics, slightly better maps, and a good
introductory reading list (but not so good on tourist information) is:

Handbooks and guides

General handbooks (cont'd.)

> Ibero-Amerika Verein, Hamburg: Ibero-
> Amerika: ein Handbuch. (Hamburg,
> Übersee-Verlag, 7 editions, 1952-70) -
> unfortunately less regularly revised than
> the S.A. handbook.

Tourist guides

There are quite a few guides more tourist-orientated than
the above. Commonest in U.K. libraries is probably
Fodor's South America (Hodder and Stoughton, annual). The
budget conscious are catered to in what Arnold and Harriet
Greenberg started in 1966 as South America on five dollars
a day (New York, Frommer, annual), but the price in the
title has since had to be raised. The motorist can rely (at
least to Panamá) on the American Automobile Association's
Mexico and Central America (revised every autumn).

Individual countries

Space precludes our detailing guides to individual countries
(but see the section 'NATIONAL BIBLIOGRAPHY' for how
to search further). We shall however mention the West
Indies and Caribbean yearbook (Skinner, annual since 1926),
a publication with strong emphasis on commercial information, and the Nagel travel guides, almost the only international series to issue volumes on individual Latin American countries (so far published: Brazil and Mexico).

Directories

These have a section on their own; see: 'DIRECTORIES'.

Handbooks and guides

Guides for students

A short guide written specially for students visiting the region is:

> Council on international educational exchange:
> **Student guide to Latin America.**   (New York,
> Dutton, 1977).

[LH]

INTER-LIBRARY LENDING

The time factor

Most disappointments with the inter-library lending system occur, not because works fail to arrive, but because they do not arrive in time to be of use. Some delay is inevitable, so you must plan your reading well in advance and make your needs known at the earliest possible moment. The following hints should also help you speed things up.

Bibliographic details

Always note where your reference came from. If your source is something at all unusual, make a photocopy of the reference: very often the British Library Lending Division (the coordinating body for inter-library loans) will insist upon proof of this sort that what you are asking for really exists.

Find out full bibliographic details: author or editor (unless it is a periodical), title (as on titlepage, not cover or spine), city or town where published, publisher, and date of publication (for a book published in the current year, or any periodical, that should mean month as well as year) - plus volume number when applicable.

The problem of discovering the author when only the title is known is dealt with under 'CATALOGUES AND INDEXES'. Periodical citation is discussed under 'PERIODICALS'.

Remember that looking for a work under a wrong or unusual style of author heading is the commonest reason for library staff failing to locate an inter-library loan request. This applies particularly to works of joint, multiple or corporate authorship (see: 'CATALOGUES & INDEXES ...'). Unfortunately libraries themselves are not consistent: depending on the exact circumstances of publication and the idiosyncrasies of the individual library, a set of conference papers (for example) may be recorded under its title, or that of the conference (in English or in the language of the country where it was held), under the sponsoring organisation, under

Bibliographic details (cont'd.)

the editor or compiler of the published papers - or under
whoever happens to have written the first paper in the book.
The safest procedure is to check the form of heading used
in the British National Bibliography (for a British publication), or in the United States National Union Catalog (for a
North American, Latin American or other foreign publication), and follow this. Even then, if the B.N.B. or N.U.C.
heading seems in any way unusual or perverse, point out any
alternative heading to the library staff when you hand in your
request.

If the work exists in several editions, decide whether you
need one particular one. If not, give details of the first, or
earliest acceptable, edition and add "or any later ed.".

Locations

You will speed your request up considerably if you can mark
it with the name of a library or libraries that you are sure
possess the item and will lend it.

To do this, write, telephone or visit the BRITISH UNION
CATALOGUE OF LATIN AMERICANA (q.v.) asking them if
they have any locations recorded for the item you seek. If
they have none, then there are still some published works
you can consult, but only if what you want is a serial or
periodical:

> Committee on Latin America: Latin American
> serials. (London, Bingley etc., distributed by
> Latin America Books of York, 1969-   ) - so
> far published: volumes on "Economic and
> social serials", "History with politics" and
> "Language, literature, art and music";

> British union catalogue of periodicals. (London,
> Butterworths, 1955-58, with a continuing series
> of supplements, currently quarterly with annual
> and five-yearly cumulations);

Locations (cont'd.)

> **British Library. Lending Division: Current serials received.** (Boston Spa, the Library, 1975, with a new edition projected every two years).

Submitting your request

If you have discovered a location or locations, you can now submit your request, telling your library staff what the locations are and how you found them.

Time will be saved if you make your request at a university library because universities can cut through the inter-library loan procedure in ways not permitted to public libraries. However, remember that the lending library may well make it a condition that its property not be lent for home reading, so make your request at a library where it is easy for you to spend time if necessary consulting the work on the premises.

Optimum time for a request where you supply the location is about two weeks. If the work happens to be out on loan when the lending library gets your request, then you can add another two weeks at least to your waiting time.

British Library Lending Division

If neither BUCLA (BRITISH UNION CATALOGUE OF LATIN AMERICANA) nor the three serial lists mentioned supply a location, then there is a fair chance the title does not exist anywhere in the country. If so, and provided it is still in print, your best course now is to ask your library staff to purchase it for you. Do this through a senior librarian who can give you an idea whether your suggestion is likely to be acceded to. Even then a work published in Latin America will still take some time to arrive (see: 'Getting books from Latin America', the penultimate paragraph of our section on 'LIBRARY FACILITIES').

Inter-library lending

British Library Lending Division   (cont'd.)

If your library is unwilling to purchase, or if it appears purchase will take too long, you can now hand in your request for an inter-library loan stating that BUCLA/COLA/BUCOP/BLLD Current serials have no locations. It will then go to the British Library Lending Division at Boston Spa. They may have it in their own stock (particularly if it is published by an American university press), or they may have a location in their own nation-wide union catalogue (this is an enormous file which does not cover all libraries, and, by its sheer size, can never be completely up-to-date). If so, the book should come in one to four weeks (if there is no waiting list): 50 per cent are supplied within 6 days. Otherwise there is always an outside chance BLLD may decide to buy a copy themselves, which will take somewhat longer.

International loan

If Boston Spa have no record of your title and no wish to purchase a copy, they will then spend about two months writing round to likely libraries. If this proves unsuccessful, the remaining possibility is for them to try overseas.

When you made your original request, you should have been asked whether, in the event of failure to locate a copy in this country, you wanted an international loan to be attempted. (If you did not reply 'yes' - or if you were never asked - more time will now be taken up while Boston Spa asks your library to ask you whether you wish them to try abroad).

Once the wheels are set in motion, the time taken to arrange an international loan depends on which foreign country is involved, and the efficiency of their inter-library loan system. (BLLD usually ask the country of publication, but sometimes try elsewhere, e.g. the USA). Although one month is not unknown, five to six months is more usual, and anything up to three years is possible.

Inter-library lending

Periodical articles and short extracts

Do not request the whole of a periodical volume, or even the whole of one issue, if you only want one particular article. Often libraries are willing to supply a photocopy of an article when they may not be prepared to lend the periodical itself. The article may also exist as an offprint when no library has the original periodical.

Similarly, if you are interested in just one part or chapter of a monograph, it may prove easier to obtain a photocopy of a short extract than to borrow the whole work.

"Unwilling to lend"

Some libraries lend no material at all: the British Library Reference Division is an example. Others impose varying degrees of restriction on what may be lent. Anything classified (however arbitrarily) as a "reference book" is usually excluded, as are particularly rare, valuable or fragile items. Works too bulky for parcel post (e.g. certain atlases and census returns) are also likely to be restricted. Many libraries refuse to lend periodicals, especially the unbound issues of the current year.

Readiness to supply photocopies of extracts and periodical articles will depend on the individual library's interpretation of its obligations to the copyright owner. The copyright problem also affects libraries' willingness to lend theses.

In such cases, the only way to see the material may be to visit the library concerned in person. Conditions under which libraries admit casual visitors, their opening hours and their inter-lending practice are detailed in:

> Naylor, Bernard, and others: Directory of libraries and special collections on Latin America and the West Indies. (London, The Athlone Press, 1975) - but see also: 'LIBRARY FACILITIES'.

Inter-library lending

The cost

Libraries, by and large, have tended to provide the inter-library lending service at no cost to the reader. However, such loan costs the borrowing library around £2 and it is likely that the financial difficulties that many institutions are suffering nowadays may force some libraries to pass a part or all of this expenditure on to the reader. Even if the service remains 'free', photocopies may well be charged for - although university staff and students may be able to claim reimbursal from faculty or departmental funds in some circumstances.

Even small charges soon mount up if you make much use of the system, so be sure to make early enquiry about the scale of charges levied.

[LH]

LANGUAGE DICTIONARIES

Citation

Nowhere does library cataloguing practice appear more arbitrary and confusing, perhaps, than in its treatment of dictionaries. Many are listed under their titles, particularly if these begin with the name of the publisher, even when it is perfectly clear who is the author responsible. Many others, in contrast, continue to appear in the catalogue under the name of some long dead author, even when the text has undergone so many revisions at the hands of successive editors that little of the original can remain. We can only indicate the practice of one major library (that of the United States Congress), and enjoin you, when you fail to trace the dictionary you seek in your library's catalogue, to try, try and try again - under author, title, publisher, revisor, original title ... And if all else fails, wade through 'Dictionaries - Spanish' (or whatever) in the subject catalogue. (Some libraries provide a heading 'Dictionaries', subdivided by language and/or subject in their author catalogue).

Spanish-English bilingual dictionaries

Perhaps we should put the biggest first, although for many purposes, biggest is not always best. For the really rare word in Spanish, it may often be better to use a Spanish-Spanish rather than a bilingual dictionary, explanations frequently being more help than inexact translations.

> Cuyás, Arturo: Gran diccionario Cuyás: inglés-español, español-inglés, nueva edición, corregida y aumentada por M. Bohigas y Rossell. (Barcelona, Hymsa, 1960) - 70,000 main entries in each part. Includes many technical terms, phrases, idioms, proverbs. Spanish American usage distinguished. First published 1928. Bears no apparent relationship to Appleton's new Cuyás dictionary (New York, 1903, 5.ed., 1972), and is fuller.

Spanish-English bilingual dictionaries (cont'd.)

Cassell's Spanish-English, English-Spanish
dictionary, by Edgar Allison Peers and others.
(London, Cassell, 1959, reprinted 1964) - some
70,000 main entries to each half. Good on Am-
ericanisms, both words and idioms: indicates
which country. Definitions are on the whole
ampler than Williams, and for breadth of
coverage is perhaps the best Spanish-English
dictionary. Its failure to distinguish between
suggested translations, especially in the English-Spanish part, makes it inferior to Raventós and to the Collins' for translation into
Spanish. Accused of plagiarism of Cuyás.

Velázquez de la Cadena, Mariano: New revised
Velázquez Spanish and English dictionary:
English-Spanish, Spanish-English, revised by
Ida Navarro Hinojosa. (Chicago, Follett, 1967 -
published in U.K. by Heinemann) - 70,000 entries
in the English-Spanish half, 60,000 in the Spanish-
English. Authoritative and comprehensive. Good
for American usage (in both languages). Somewhat apt to give explanations instead of equivalents. First edition 1852.

Williams, Edwin B.: Dictionary, Spanish and
English; diccionario inglés y español. (New
York, Holt Rinehart & Winston, 1963) - just under
60,000 entries in each section. American and
European usage well distinguished. Up-to-date,
well laid out and thumb-indexed, but on the whole
neither as full as Cassell's, nor as good as Raventós in distinguishing different translations.
Praised for its coverage of scientific and technical language, but damned for the stiltedness of
its translation of colloquialisms.

Language dictionaries

Vox: diccionario inglés-español, español-inglés, por Carlos F. Mac Hale. (Barcelona, Juventud, 1964) - 60,000 English main entries, 50,000 Spanish. Preference given to European usage (in both languages). Mostly equivalents: few idioms. Odd feature is provision of elementary grammatical notes in boxes under such headings as 'Gender', 'Gerund', 'Gerundio', 'Subjuntivo'. The Spanish-English half is distinguished by tinted paper.

Magnus diccionario inglés-español, Spanish-English, 5.ed. (Buenos Aires, Sopena, 1965) - 50,000 main entries in each section. Preference given to Argentine and United States usage.

Best for translating into Spanish are:

Collins' Spanish-English, English-Spanish dictionary, by [Christopher] Colin Smith and others. (London, Collins, 1971) - only about 40,000 main entries in each section, but by deliberately omitting the "lexicographical lumber" of archaisms, recondite technical terms and readily deducible derivatives, Smith has given himself room to provide adequate treatment of the vocabulary of "the average educated person". High frequency words ('de', 'dar', 'go', 'for' etc.) particularly well covered. Familiar, slang, obscene and American usage well catered for, but more in the Spanish than in the English half. Choice between alternatives always clear. Particularly good on colloquial equivalents. Slight bias towards European usage. Reviewed in Hispania, 56(2), 1973, pp.511-521 under title "A landmark in bilingual lexicography", and for many purposes clearly the best Spanish dictionary, as well as being the latest.

Language dictionaries

Spanish-English bilingual dictionaries (cont'd.)

Langenscheidt's standard dictionary of the
English and Spanish languages: English-Spanish,
Spanish-English. (London, Hodder and Stoughton,
1966) - 15,000 main entries in the English half,
14,000 in the Spanish. Also by Christopher Colin
Smith (and others) and many of the ideas govern-
ing the Collins' were first tried out here. Syl-
labification of English entries. 'Reliable small
dictionary for desk use'.

Raventós, Margaret H.: The E.U.P. modern
Spanish dictionary: Spanish-English, English-
Spanish. (London, English Universities Press,
1968) - "Teach yourself books" reprint of her
Modern Spanish dictionary (published in New
York as McKay's modern Spanish-English,
English-Spanish dictionary), textually unabridged
but photographically reduced (slightly) in print
size. 27,000 entries in Spanish half, 32,000 in
English. Omits obsolete, regional (including
Spanish American) and specialised technical
terms, but is good on modern words (e.g. 'pres-
sure cooker') and on idioms. Choice between
different translations clearly indicated. Ideal for
the learner, and, in its "Teach yourself" format,
by far the lowest-priced, good dictionary.

Especially good for the spoken language:

United States of America. War Department:
Dictionary of spoken Spanish: Spanish-English,
English-Spanish. (Washington, GPO, 1945, reprinted New York, Dover, 1958) - originally produced in wartime for the U.S. army, emphasises
the colloquial and the practical, with many
examples. American usage (in both languages).

Language dictionaries

Portuguese-English bilingual dictionaries

We particularly recommend:

> Taylor, James L.: A Portuguese-English diction-
> ary, revised. (Stanford, Stanford University
> Press, 1970; London, Harrap) - 65,000 entries.
> Hailed on its first appearance in 1958 as the
> "Most complete and accurate of Portuguese bi-
> lingual dictionaries". Good on idioms and tech-
> nical terms, especially for Brazilian flora and
> fauna. A one-way dictionary, intended to comple-
> ment a work such as:

> Vallandro, Leonel, and Vallandro, Lino: Dicionário
> inglês-português. 3.ed. (Porto Alegre, Globo,
> 1976) - nearly 60,000 entries. English-Portuguese
> only. Like Taylor, mainly American usage (in both
> languages).

The longest running Portuguese bilingual dictionary has
been:

> Michaelis, Henriette: Novo Michaelis dicionário
> ilustrado. Inglês-português. Português-inglês.
> (São Paulo, Melhoramentos, 2 vols, 1958-61;
> Wiesbaden, Brockhaus) - 73,000 entries in the
> Portuguese half, somewhat less in the English vol-
> ume. The work in its original form dates back to
> 1893.

The newest one is:

> Houaiss, Antonio, and Avery, C.B.: New Appleton
> dictionary of the English and Portuguese lan-
> guages. (New York, Appleton-Century-Crofts,
> 1964, reprinted 1967) - 60,000 entries in each half.
> As Houaiss had the temerity to translate Joyce's
> Ulysses he should prove a most competent lexico-
> grapher!

Language dictionaries

Portuguese-English bilingual dictionaries (cont'd.)

A useful compact dictionary, but with emphasis on European usage:

> Ferreira, Julio Albino: Dicionário português-inglês, inglês-português, nova edição, revista e melhorada pelo dr. Armando de Morais. (Oporto, Domingos Barreira, 2 vols, 1951-54).

Technical and other dictionaries

Space precludes any listing of technical dictionaries. Two standard guides are:

> Collison, Robert L.W.: Dictionaries of English and foreign languages. (London, Hafner, 1971) - and

> Walford, Albert J. and Screes, J.E.O.: A guide to foreign language courses and dictionaries, 3.ed. (London, Library Association, 1977).

Spanish and Portuguese technical dictionaries held by Canning House Library are catalogued in:

> Hispanic and Luso-Brazilian Council, London. Library: Portuguese and Spanish dictionaries. (London, The Council, 1971).

Libraries in the Ealing and Acton areas of West London have produced a useful union list:

> Coöperative industrial and commercial reference information service: Union list of interlingual dictionaries, 2.ed. (Acton, Acton Public Library for CICRIS, 1971).

The editor is compiling a card file of Portuguese dictionaries and glossaries and would be pleased to answer enquiries not satisfied by the above, in respect of that language.

[LH]

LAW & LEGISLATION

Thirty differing systems of law

Eighteen republics and the associated state of Puerto Rico draw their law from that of Spain. Brazil has a Portuguese legal heritage. Haiti has naturally drawn on the Code Napoléon. In Surinam and Guiana law has a Dutch Roman origin. The five other independent Commonwealth countries are outside the Roman tradition altogether, having a basis of English Common Law ... Clearly anyone who needs to delve much into such a maze will soon need the guidance of an experienced law librarian, such as those on the staff of the London Institute of Advanced Legal Studies Library. The following may provide some initial help.

Introductory

A brief introduction to the complexities of the field is the article:

> Figueredo, Fernando J.: "Acquisition of Latin American legal materials, a burdensome task", Fifteenth Seminar on the Acquisition of Latin American Library Materials, Toronto, 1970 (Working paper 10).

More detailed surveys are:

> Clagett, Helen L.: Administration of justice in Latin America. (New York, Oceana, 1952) - and:

> DeVries, Henry P., and Rodríguez Novás, José: The law of the Americas, an introduction to the legal systems of the American republics. (Dobbs Ferry, Oceana, 1965),

while for Brazil there is a useful chapter by Anyda Marchant, "The political and legal framework of Brazilian life" on pp.96-132 of:

Law & Legislation

Introductory (cont'd.)

> Modern Brazil, new patterns and development,
> edited by John Saunders. (Gainesville, Uni-
> versity of Florida Press, 1971).

Peru is covered in:

> Valderrama, David M.: Law and legal literature of
> Peru: a revised guide. (Washington, GPO for Lib-
> rary of Congress, 1977) - based on a 1947 work by
> Helen L. Clagett.

A brief note on Cuban law material is Armando E. González's
"Law materials" on pp.73-77 of:

> International conference on Cuban acquisition and
> bibliography, Library of Congress, Washington,
> 1970: Cuban acquisitions and bibliography, proceed-
> ings and working papers ..., edited by Earl J.
> Pariseau. (Washington, Hispanic Foundation of
> the Library of Congress, 1970).

General outlines of actual law are most easily accessible in
the pamphlet series Statement of the laws ... in matters affecting business (which are somewhat wider in scope than
their titles suggest). These have been published on a basis of
one for each OAS member, with rather irregular revision, for
some decades past by the General legal division of the Pan
American Union (now become the Department of legal affairs
of the Organization of American States).

Bibliographies

Limited to works in English are:

> Bayitch, Stojan A.: Guide to inter-American legal aff-
> airs. (Coral Gables, Law Library of the University of
> Miami, 1957) - revised and incorporated in:

> Bayitch, Stojan A.: Latin America, a bibliographical
> guide to economy, history, law, politics and society.
> (Coral Gables, University of Miami Press, 1961) -
> which led on to his:

Law & legislation

Bibliographies (cont'd.)

> Bayitch, Stojan A.: Latin America and the Caribbean, a bibliographical guide to works in English. (Coral Gables, University of Miami; Dobbs Ferry, Oceana, 1967).

Not so linguistically restricted are:

> American Association of Law Libraries. Committee on foreign and international law: Union list of basic Latin American legal materials, edited by Kate Wallach. (South Hackensack, Rothman, 1971);

> Rank, Richard: The criminal justice systems of the Latin American nations: a bibliography of the primary and secondary literature. (South Hackensack, Criminal law education and research center of New York University, 1974);

> Villalón Galdames, Alberto: Bibliografía jurídica de América latina 1810-1965. (Santiago de Chile, Jurídica, 5 vols planned, 1969-   ) - only vol 1, "Argentina y Bolivia", so far published.

There is also a recent work on West Indian material:

> Patchett, Keith, and Jenkins, V.: A bibliographical guide to law in the Commonwealth Caribbean. (Mona, Institute of social and economic research of the University of the West Indies, 1973).

Indexes

Thirty Latin American legal periodicals are included in:

> Index to foreign legal periodicals, 1960-   (London, Institute of advanced legal studies, 1964-   ) - quarterly, with annual and triennial cumulation;

Law & legislation

Indexes   (cont'd.)

and new laws are indexed in:

> United States of America. Library of Congress.
> Hispanic Law Division: Index to Latin American
> legislation, 1950-   (Boston, Hall, 1961-   ) -
> two vols covering to 1960, continued by five-yearly
> supplements.

Official gazettes

Official gazettes are an important source for the texts of
new legal instruments and much other legal information.
For details consult the sources referred to in the paragraph
'Bibliographies' in the section on 'OFFICIAL PUBLICA-
TIONS'.

Since the autumn of 1974, the U.S. Library of Congress has
begun producing microfilms of all its Latin American
official gazettes: your library will advise whether it is possible to obtain these.

Citation

Political sovereignties are regarded in library catalogues
as the authors of their own laws. Thus you look for the text
of any legal instrument under the name of the appropriate
country, state, province or other jurisdiction, except that
the laws of England, Scotland and Northern Ireland are usually all lumped together under Great Britain: the effect,
presumably, of ignorance of British political niceties on the
part of the Yankee librarians who drew the rules up.

The constitutional law of each country (or other political
entity) has the subheading 'constitution', with possible sub-
division by date. Thus the constitution of Vargas's Estado
novo would be under 'Brazil. Constitution. 1937'.

Citation   (cont'd.)

All other forms of law, whether they be acts of the legislature, presidential decrees, ministerial orders or what-
have-you, are grouped together under the subheading Laws,
or an appropriate variant (e.g. 'Great Britain. Laws,
statutes etc.', or - in a Brazilian catalogue - 'Brasil. Leis,
decretos etc.').

Headings such as 'Brazil. Congresso' exist, and include
records of debates, reports of congressional committees
and the texts of proposed legislation ('bills' in Anglo-
American terminology), but not any promulgated statutes.
Similarly, 'Peru. Presidente' will cover official messages
from the head of state to the nation or the Congress, but
will not be used for presidential decrees.

International agreements are usually indexed under their
name in English: e.g. 'Montevideo treaty' or 'Treaty for
the prohibition of muclear weapons in Latin America, 1967';
but bilateral agreements are usually cited by the name of
one of the signatory sovereignties, subheaded 'Treaties':
e.g. the Treaty of Guadalupe Hidalgo which ended the U.S.-
Mexican War would be found as:

> Mexico. Treaties etc. 1848: Tratado de paz,
> amistad y limites entre la República mexi-
> cana y los Estados unidos de América.

[LH]

LIBRARY FACILITIES

University libraries

The five "Parry centres" of Latin American studies (the
universities of Cambridge, Glasgow, Liverpool, London and
Oxford) were given special funds by the University Grants
Committee to develop their library collections in this field.
The University of Essex has also devoted substantial resources to developing a sound research collection on Latin
America. Each of these universities therefore has strong
library facilities for Latin American studies and, even if
the collection may not be specifically arranged for the im-
mediate convenience of the Latin Americanist, there will
usually be someone on the library staff experienced in the
region. Since none of the collections can be comprehensive,
each has usually concentrated in some measure on certain
countries or fields of study. They have collaborated to try
to share out their strengths and prevent any areas or topics
being neglected - particularly in the case of the constituent
libraries of the University of London - but academic pre-
ferences and limited resources have reduced the effective-
ness of this.

Several of these universities have Centres or Institutes of
Latin American Studies, some with their own libraries. In
almost every case however, the bulk of the collection is kept
in the main university library and the centre (or institute)
has just a small working collection for students. The special
role of the London Institute of Latin American Studies library is explained in the section 'BRITISH UNION CATA-
LOGUE OF LATIN AMERICANA'.

Some other university libraries have noteworthy collections
in certain subject fields (e.g. in Latin American economic
development at the University of Sussex Institute of Development Studies), but it is generally the case that, outside the
"Parry centres" and Essex, coverage of Latin America is
poorer and more selective. It is usually meant to meet the
teaching and research requirements of members of the
academic staff with an interest in the region. It is almost

University libraries (cont'd.)

certainly not organised with the aim of serving the general
needs of Latin Americanists, and the library staff, although
well equipped with general bibliographical expertise, will
probably lack specialist knowledge. These collections are
not coördinated with each other, nor with the collections of
the six major centres.

Polytechnic libraries

The Polytechnic libraries of Portsmouth and Wolverhampton
and the library of Ealing College of Further Education in
West London have started from a much poorer base but have
made significant efforts to develop good collections to support their special interests in Latin American studies. In
organisation and provision of specialist librarian support
they resemble the six major university libraries, but they
cannot match the latter's strength of holdings.

The British Library

The national library offers some facilities which supplement
those just described. The Reference division has the United
Kingdom's biggest general Latin American collection in
what used to be the British Museum Library; although there
are many significant gaps, the holdings are strong in depth
and in breadth. The government publications are especially
noteworthy. Its published catalogue is available in many
libraries, but its resources may not be borrowed through
inter-library loan. The same restriction applies to the
Division's Science Reference Library, which aims to be
comprehensive within its fields of interest (see 'Science
and technology' in the section 'SUBJECT BIBLIOGRAPHY -
MAJOR SUBJECTS').

The British Library's Lending Division at Boston Spa, near
Wetherby, Yorkshire, combines the former National Lending
Library for Science and Technology and National Central
Library. It exists to supply material to other libraries on

Library facilities

The British Library (cont'd.)

inter-library loan, either in the original or in photocopy (see: 'INTER LIBRARY LENDING') and provides a return-of-post service for material in its own stock. It is an important source of THESES (q.v.) and acquires almost all U.S. academic press publications. It is specially strong in recent periodicals, and claims to acquire all those cited in the current Handbook of Latin American studies. (In case of any difficulty with Latin American scientific and technical periodicals, however, remember that these are also subscribed to intensively by the Science Reference Library).

Special libraries

Many other libraries have material of Latin American interest. There are, for instance, many specialist libraries which collect material on the Latin American aspects of their subject, be it taxation, meteorology or crime, as part of their attempt to be comprehensive within their own subject. Many of them are in London.

For further information about these and other libraries, consult:

> Naylor, Bernard, and others: Directory of libraries and special collections on Latin America and the West Indies. (London, Athlone Press for the Institute of Latin American Studies, 1975) - a geographical listing of U.K. libraries with a subject index.

Also of use:

> Great Britain. Science reference library: Guide to government department and other libraries and information bureaux. (London, British Library, 1976);

> Irwin, Raymond, and Staveley, R.: The libraries of London, 2.ed. (London, The Library Association, 1961);

Special libraries (cont'd.)

> Morgan, Paul: Oxford libraries outside the
> Bodleian. (Oxford, Oxford Bibliographical
> Society, and The Bodleian Library, 1973);
>
> Commonwealth Institute, London. Working party
> on library holdings of Commonwealth literature:
> A handbook of library holdings of Commonwealth
> literature in the United Kingdom, compiled and
> edited by Gail Wilson. (London, The Working
> Party, 1971).

Borrowing from other libraries

Most libraries will admit bona fide researchers as readers,
although very few will extend borrowing privileges outside
their normal membership. The Naylor Directory (above)
indicates libraries' policies in these respects. Students
should first obtain SCONUL/COPOL vacation reading cards
from their own institutions as identification.

Procedures for getting books and other material on loan
from the British Library Lending Division and elsewhere
are explained in the section on 'INTER LIBRARY LENDING!

Getting books from Latin America

If your library is unable to borrow an item you want, it may
be prepared to make a special purchase. The library staff
will tell you how to go about requesting this: make your ap-
plication through a senior librarian, who will be able to give
you some idea whether the suggestion is likely to be agreed
to. If it is something published in a Latin American country,
you must be prepared for a long wait. Dealers in this
country can only stock a small fraction of Latin American
publishing output, and either they or your library will often
have to order specially from the place of publication. Since
airmail is too expensive, it may take from six weeks to six
months from the placing of the order to the receipt of the

Library facilities

Getting books from Latin America (cont'd.)

item. Other problems, such as short print-runs and in-adequate distribution networks, may further complicate supply. If the dealer has to wait for a reprint, or if he had to search for a second-hand copy of an out-of-print title, six months can easily be exceeded. For the library user, the lesson is clear: books not already in the United Kingdom will probably be a long, long time coming. Therefore, plan your reading well ahead, and give your library the earliest possible notice of the books (etc.) your research will require.

Dealing with library staff

As librarians, we naturally hope all your dealings with the profession are happy ones. Experience however tells us that a few elementary points may be worth making.

Firstly, get acquainted with your library's hierarchy, so that you can choose the appropriate level for every contact: do not seek out the chief librarian when all you want to know is the library's opening hours, nor expect the girl on the issue desk to know details of the British Library's latest moves in computerised information services. Find out whether the staff includes a Latin Americanist, and get to know him, or her.

Secondly, make every request as precise and specific as possible; e.g. do not ask "What does the library have on West Indian political parties?" when what you really want is to compare the voting strength of PNM in rural areas of South Trinidad between the elections of 1956 and 1966.

Thirdly, remember that, however extended a library's opening hours may be, it almost certainly operates on a skeleton staff outside normal Monday to Friday office hours. Try to raise all your difficult problems on weekdays, and well before five o'clock.

[BN]

LIBRARY FACILITIES ABROAD

North America

For general information on Latin American collections in the U.S. and Canada, see:

> Haro, Robert P.: Latin American research in the United States and Canada: a guide and directory. (Chicago, American Library Association, 1971).

The major collections are discussed in some detail by:

> Jackson, William V., ed.: Latin American collections. (Nashville, Vanderbilt University Bookstore, 1974).

Jackson was also responsible for:

> Jackson, William V.: Library guide for Brazilian studies. (Pittsburgh, University of Pittsburgh Book Center, 1964).

Spain

Whilst Spain's largest collection of American material is in the Biblioteca nacional in Madrid (much of it, but by no means all, in its Sección de Hispanoamérica), contemporary Latin America is perhaps better studied in the Biblioteca Hispánica of the Instituto de Cultura Hispánica (also in Madrid). This possesses some 400,000 volumes and over 6,000 periodical titles. Next in importance perhaps come the libraries of the various institutes of the Consejo Superior de Investigaciones Científicas.

Important within their respective specialities are the libraries of the Museo Naval, of the Servicio Histórico Militar and of the Jesuits, Franciscans and other missionary orders.

Provincial universities with large American collections include Seville (Biblioteca de la Escuela de Estudios Hispanoamericanos) and Santiago de Compostela (Biblioteca de América).

Library facilities abroad

West Germany

The largest library in Europe specialising in Latin America is that of the Preussischer Kulturbesitz's Ibero-Amerikanisches Institut, in West Berlin, with almost half a million volumes, an intake of 6,500 current periodicals, a newspaper clippings file started in 1930, 30,000 maps, 5,000 records and tapes, a photographic library and a collection of Brazilian popular art. Its catalogue is being published by G.K. Hall (see: 'PRINTED CATALOGUES'). Germany's most important centre for research on the region outside Berlin is Hamburg, where several institutions (the oldest dating from 1917) contribute to a union catalogue that now exceeds 130,000 entries. Further details from:

> Siefer, Elisabeth: Neuere Deutsche Lateinamerika-Forschung Institute und Bibliotheken in der Bundesrepublik Deutschland und in Berlin (West). (Hamburg, Arbeitsgemeinschaft Deutsche Lateinamerika-Forschung, 1971).

Portugal

> Boschi, Caio César: "O Brasil nos arquivos e bibliotecas de Portugal: levantamento bibliográfico crítico dos arquivos e bibliotecas de Portugal úteis ao pesquisador da história do Brasil", Revista de história (São Paulo), 51(101), 1975, pp.343-400;

> Pescatello, Ann: "Relatório from Portugal: the archives and libraries of Portugal and their significance for the study of Brazilian history", Latin American research review, 5(2), Summer 1970, pp.17-52.

Library facilities abroad

Latin America

The Organization of American States' Columbus memorial library issued a memeographed Guía de bibliotecas de la América latina in 1963. More recent is:

Hilton, Ronald: The scientific institutions of Latin America, with special reference to their organization and facilities. (Stanford, Institute of international studies, 1970) - and:

Instituto brasileiro de bibliografia e documentação: Guía de bibliotecas especializadas e centros de documentação da América latina. (Rio de Janeiro, the Institute, 1971).

A selection of the larger libraries of the region (and elsewhere in the world) is discussed in:

Steele, Colin R.: Major libraries of the world, a selective guide. (London etc., Bowker, 1976).

Very good for giving the 'feel' of how libraries are run in Latin America, even though its coverage is limited to just two countries, is:

McCarthy, Cavan: Developing libraries in Brazil, with a chapter on Paraguay. (Metuchen, Scarecrow, 1975).

More formal accounts will be found in the articles "Argentina, libraries in", "Bolivia, libraries in", "Brazil, libraries in" ... "El Salvador, national library in", etc., in the Encyclopedia of library and information science, edited by Allen Kent and others (New York, Dekker, 1968-   ), which is still in process of publication.

[LH]

MANUSCRIPTS & ARCHIVES

General

Gropp, Arthur E.: "Bibliografia de fuentes archi-
vísticas relacionadas con Ibero-América: catálogos, guías, índices, inventorios, listas y publicaciones periódicas", Anuario de estudios
americanos, 12, 1965, pp.919-973.

In the British Isles

A UNESCO plan for a series of national "Guides to the
sources of the history of Latin America" has so far been
fulfilled for Italy, the Vatican City, East and West Germany,
the Low Countries, Scandinavia, Spain, the U.S.A. and the
British Isles. Each volume is published separately by the
respective National Commissions, although all but the first
two have also been made available in microfiche by the Inter
Documentation Company of Zug in Switzerland. Our contribution is:

Walne, Peter: A guide to manuscript sources for
the history of Latin America and the Caribbean
in the British Isles. (London, Oxford University
Press, 1973) - an encyclopaedic guide of extra-
ordinary width, detail and interest, listing government, county, city, private and business collections.
It omits however items cited in:

British Museum. Department of manuscripts.
Catalogue of the manuscripts in the Spanish language in the British Museum, by don Pascual de
Gayangos [y Arce]. (London, the Museum, 4 vols,
1875-93, reprinted 1976).

Mexican materials in London are particularly well favoured,
by three recent works:

In the British Isles (cont'd.)

Grajales Ramos, Gloria: Guía de documentos para
la historia de México existentes en la Public
Record Office de Londres, 1827-1830. (Mexico
City, Comisión de historia del Instituto panamericano de geografía e historia, 1967) - includes
diplomatic correspondence and correspondence
from the Foreign Office Archive relating to trade
in the formative years of the Republic;

Grajales Ramos, Gloria: Guía de documentos para
la historia de México en archivos ingleses, siglo
diez y nueve. (Mexico City, UNAM, 1969) - des-
cribes documents in the Public Record Office and
the British Museum;

Costeloe, Michael P.: Mexico state papers 1744-
1843: a descriptive catalogue of the G.R.G. Con-
way Collection in the Institute of Historical
Research, University of London. (London, Athlone
Press, 1976) - a collection of 1200 items touching
many major events in late colonial and early independent Mexico. Only a few are in manuscript, but
since almost all exist nowhere outside this collection
it seems appropriate to include it here.

A Catálogo dos manuscriptos portugueses existentes no
Museo Britannico, most of which are of Brazilian interest,
was compiled by Frederico Francisco Stuart de Figanière,
and published in Lisbon as far back as 1853. Ten years
later "F.A.V." (the initials of the Brazilian historian
Vernhagen) supplemented this with his Succinta indicação de
alguns manuscriptos importantes ... não comprehendidos no
catalogo Figanière. Both works were later corrected and
added to by:

Manuscripts & archives

In the British Isles (cont'd.)

> Lima, Manuel de Oliveira: "Relação dos manu-
> scriptos portugueses e estrangeiros de interesse
> para o Brazil, existentes no Museu Britannico de
> Londres", Revista trimestral do Instituto histó-
> rico e geográfico brasileiro, 65(2), 1902, pp.5-
> 139 - also published separately, Rio de Janeiro,
> 1903.

Spain

For a first introduction:

> Burrus, Ernest J.: "An introduction to the biblio-
> graphic tools in Spanish archives and manuscript
> collections relating to Hispanic America", His-
> panic American historical review, 35, 1955,
> pp.443-483.

and for the older material:

> Freudenthal, Juan B.: "Early colonial archives
> in Spain: key to research about Spanish America,"
> SALALM Newsletter, 5(1), March 1977, pp.5-6.

Other general guides are:

> Spain. Dirección general de archivos y biblio-
> tecas: Guía de fuentes para la historia de Ibero-
> América conservados en España. (Madrid, the
> Dirección, 2 vols, 1966-69) - Spain's contribution
> to the UNESCO project mentioned above. It does, how-
> ever, only partly supercede the older and less in-
> clusive but rather more detailed:

> Tudela, José: Los manuscritos de América en las
> bibliotecas de España. (Madrid, Ediciones
> Cultura hispánica, 1954) - extremely detailed and
> interesting entries.

Spain (cont'd.)

Two repositories stand out as goals for colonial researchers, the Archivo general de Indias in Seville, and the
Archivo general at Simancas, neither of which enjoys a
recent, detailed guide to its resources. Of what does exist,
the best guides to the former are:

> Bermúdez Plata, Cristóbal: El Archivo general
> de Indias de Sevilla, sede del americanismo.
> (Madrid, Cuerpo facultativo de archiveros, bib-
> liotecarios y arqueólogos, 1951) - lacks contents
> list and index, but is a useful short general guide
> to the papers and the history of their deposit; and:

> Spain. Archivo general de Indias, Seville: Archivo
> general de Indias de Sevilla, guía de visitante, por
> José María de la Peña y de la Cámara. (Madrid,
> Dirección general de archivos y bibliotecas, 1958,) -
> although not intended for specialists, does provide
> important information on the major classes of
> material and refers to the printed descriptive
> material on various sections of the Archive.

Simancas, whose American documents largely arrived in the
late 19th century, and which are primarily concerned with
matters of imperial defence in the latter half of the 18th and
early 19th centuries (but have also much on, e.g. comercio
libre, is served by the official:

> Spain. Archivo general de Simancas: Guía del
> Archivo general de Simancas. (Madrid,
> Dirección general de archivos y bibliotecas,
> 1958).

For Madrid there is:

> Spain. Dirección general de archivos y biblio-
> tecas: Guía de los archivos de Madrid. (Madrid,
> Servicio de publicaciones del Ministerio de edu-
> cación nacional, 1951).

Manuscripts & archives

Portugal

The latest of several guides to Brazilian material in Portuguese archives is:

> Boschi, Caio César: "O Brasil nos arquivos e bibliotecas de Portugal: levantamento bibliográfico crítico dos arquivos e bibliotecas de Portugal úteis ao pesquisador da história do Brasil", Revista de historia (São Paulo), 51 (101), 1975, pp.343-400;

More accessible perhaps is:

> Pescatello, Ann: "Relatório from Portugal: the archives and libraries of Portugal and their significance for the study of Brazilian history", Latin American research review, 5(2), Summer 1970, pp.17-52.

The rest of Europe

A useful starting point is the general guide to archives published in the journal History from October 1968, beginning with a guide to German archives by J.R.C.Wright. A more detailed approach is adopted in:

> Thomas, Daniel H., and Case, L.M., ed.: The new guide to the diplomatic archives of Western Europe. (Philadelphia, University of Pennsylvania Press, 1975) - revising their original Guide of 1959; and:

> Gómez Canedo, Lino: Los archivos de la historia de América: período colonial español. (México, Instituto panamericano de geografía e historia, 2 vols, 1961) - a remarkably complete survey.

The Instituto panamericano de geografía e historia is also responsible for the series Misiones americanas en los archivos europeos, begun in 1949, which covers most of the

Manuscripts & archives

(cont'd.)

modern archival explorations carried out in European archives by individual Latin American countries.

Surveys of resources in individual countries include:

Burrus, Ernest J.: "Research opportunities in Italian archives and manuscript collections for students of Hispanic American history", Hispanic American historical review, 39, 1959, pp.428-463;

Gavrilovic, S.: "Hispanic American history research opportunities in Yugoslav archives", Hispanic American Historical Review, 42(1), 1962, pp.37-50;

German Democratic Republic. Staatliche Archivverwaltung: Übersicht über die Quellen zur Geschichte Lateinamerikas in Archiven der Deutschen Demokratischen Republik. (Potsdam, 1971);

Hauschild-Thiessen, Renate, and Bachmann, E.: Führer durch die Quellen zur Geschichte Lateinamerikas in der Bundesrepublik Deutschlands. (Bremen, Schüneman, 1972);

Liagre, Léone, and Baerten, J.: Guide des sources de l'histoire d'Amérique latine conservées en Belgique. (Brussels, Archives généraux du royaume, 1967);

Lodolini, Elio: Guida delle fonti per la storia dell'America latina esistenti in Italia. (Rome, Direzione generale degli Archivo di Stato, 1976-   ) - in progress;

Mörner, Magnus: Fuentes para la historia de Ibero-América: Escandinavia. (Stockholm, Riksarkivet, 1968) - another contribution to the UNESCO project;

The rest of Europe (cont'd.)

Ozanam, Didier: Guide du chercheur dans les
archives françaises: les sources de l'histoire
de l'Amérique latine. (Paris, Institut des
hautes études de l'Amérique latine, 1963-   ) -
in progress;

Pásztor, Lajos: Guida delle fonte per la storia
dell'America latina negli archivi della Santa
Sede e negli archivi ecclesiastici d'Italia.
(Vatican City, Archivo vaticano, 1970);

Roessingh, M.P.H.: Guide to the sources in the
Netherlands for the history of Latin America.
(The Hague, Algemeen Rijksarchief, 1968).

North America

With nearly 400 institutions interested in Latin America, the
U.S.A. possesses probably the widest range of original
sources on this theme in the world. General guides include:

Bartley, Russell H., and Wagner, S.L.: Latin
America in basic historical collections: a
working guide. (Stanford, Hoover Institution,
1972) - although best on the U.S.A. (107 institutions), it also covers Canada, Latin America,
Europe, Australia, Japan, the Philippines and
the West Indies. There is also a large bibliography (875 items), and a brief note on data
banks.

Hilton, Ronald: Handbook of Hispanic source
materials and research organizations in the
United States, 2.ed. (Stanford University
Press, 1956).

Manuscripts & archives

North America (cont'd.)

Thirteen major collections are discussed in some detail in:

> Jackson, William V., ed.: Latin American collections. (Nashville, Vanderbilt University Bookstore, 1974).

The most important of the guides to individual collections are probably:

> United States of America. National archives and records service: Guide to materials on Latin America in the National archives of the United States, by George S. Ulibarri and J.P. Harrison. (Washington, G.P.O., 1974) - revision of a 1961 work by Harrison;

> Spell, Lota M.: Research materials for the study of Latin America at the University of Texas. (Austin, University of Texas Press, 1954, reprinted Westport, Conn., Greenwood, 1970) - page 18 refers to the catalogues in print on important archival collections in Europe and Latin America.

Sources of material on the Commonwealth Caribbean are set out in:

> Ingram, Kenneth E.: Manuscripts relating to Commonwealth Caribbean countries in United States and Canadian repositories. (Epping, Essex, Bowker, for Caribbean Universities Press, 1975).

Manuscripts & archives

Latin America

The general guides are:

Hill, Roscoe R.: The national archives of Latin
America. (Cambridge, Mass., Harvard University Press, 1945) - includes the national
collections of twenty countries, describing their
establishment, history, buildings, directors,
publishing and contents;

Gropp, Arthur E.: Guide to libraries and archives
in Central America and the West Indies, Panama,
Bermuda and British Guiana. (New Orleans,
Middle America research institute, 1941);

Millares Carlo, Agustín: Los archivos municipales
de Latinoamérica: libros de actas y collecciones
documentales; apuntes bibliográficas. (Maracaibo,
Universidad del Zulia, 1961).

Although Hill and Gropp are now rather outdated, they are
still valuable sources. More up-to-date information is only
available in the published literature of the individual countries, except for Bartley and Wagner (mentioned under
'United States of America') and:

Mendoza L., Gunnar: Situación actual de los
archivos latinoamericanos: manual de información básica. (Washington, Reunión inter-
americana sobre archivos, 1961);

Morales, Enrique L.: "Estado actual de los
archivos en Latinoamérica", Boletín de la
Escuela nacional de bibliotecarios y archi-
vistas (Mexico City), 5(28), Apr 1961/Aug
1962, pp.45-72.

Manuscripts & archives

Codices

An index to ancient Mexican codices, giving alternative titles, present location, and whether published, was begun ten years ago, but is apparently still uncompleted:

> Mateos Higuera, Salvador: "Códices picto-
> gráficos mesoamericanos", Boletín biblio-
> gráfico de la Secretaría de Hacienda y Crédito
> público, Suplemento al num. 354, Nov.1966 -
> only part so far issued, covered A-C.

Another guide to codices from what is now Mexico is:

> Azcue y Mancera, Luis: Códices indígenas.
> (Mexico City, Orion, 1966) - well organised,
> with good indexes, in particular to the country,
> city and place of deposit; and brief but infor-
> mative notes on cultures of origin: Nahuatl,
> Maya, Mixtec etc.

Rather more specialised catalogues and bibliographies are found in;

> Glass, John B.: Catálogo de la Colección de
> Códices. (Mexico City, Instituto nacional
> de antropología e historia, 1964) - full des-
> cription, history, list of copies and bibliography
> of each of the 128 manuscripts in the Museo de
> Antropología in Mexico City, with 139 plates
> and useful appendices;

> Gibson, Charles: The Aztecs under Spanish rule:
> a history of the Indians of the Valley of Mexico
> 1519-1810. (Stanford, Stanford University Press,
> 1964) - the bibliography with its introductory note,
> pp.607-634, is probably the best survey for the
> area;

Codices (cont'd.)

Robertson, Donald: Mexican manuscript painting
of the early colonial period: the metropolitan
schools. (New Haven, Yale University Press,
1959) - 'a study of a selected group of manuscripts from the Central Valley of Mexico' whose
pp.199-200 constitute a useful key to catalogues
and lists of manuscripts, and pp.203-217 the
useful general bibliography.

Two books by Miguel León-Portilla, Aztec thought and
culture, a study of the ancient Nahuatl mind (University of
Oklahoma Press, 1963) and his Precolumbian literatures
of Mexico (University of Oklahoma Press, 1969), both
translated from the Spanish, have useful bibliographies
which are to some extent guides to facsimiles and to places of deposit of the originals. There are also several
checklists and censuses of Middle American Indian manuscripts by John B. Glass and others in vols 14 and 15 of the
Handbook of Middle American Indians (University of Texas
Press, 1975), but until we have a full and detailed guide to
all American Indian manuscripts, their identification and
location will remain a rather piecemeal activity.

The West Indies

Basic information on the archives of almost all the coun-
tries of the Caribbean (including, albeit briefly, Cuba,
Mexico, Guatemala and Colombia) is available in the
Report of the Caribbean Archives Conference, held at the
University of the West Indies, Mona, Jamaica, September
20-27, 1965, under the joint sponsorship of the Government
of Jamaica and the University. Information is included on
Caribbean records held in European repositories. The
Report can be supplemented by the six-monthly bulletin of
the Caribbean Archives Association, Caribbean archives
(1973-   ), produced by the Archives de la Guadeloupe,
Basse-Terre, Guadeloupe.

The West Indies (cont'd.)

For Jamaica there is also:

> Ingram, Kenneth E.: Sources of Jamaica history,
> 1655-1838: a bibliographical survey with par-
> ticular reference to manuscript sources.
> (Zug, Inter-Documentation Company, 2 vols,
> 1976).

Archives and manuscripts on microfilm

See the section 'MICROFILM MATERIAL'.

Guides to Latin American paleography

The best, if not the only, guide to reading Latin American
manuscripts would appear to be:

> Millares Carlo, Agustín, and Mantecón, José
> Ignacio: Album de paleografía hispanoameri-
> cana de los siglos xvi y xvii.   (Mexico City,
> Instituto Panamericano de Geografía e His-
> toria, 3 pts, 1955) - no.3 of the Institute's
> Manuales de técnica de la investigación de la
> historia y ciencias afines.

One part is devoted to plates, and another to their trans-
sciption. Styles of the 18th century and later are not dealt
with, but handwriting has by then become very much easier
to decypher.

[RP]

MAPS & ATLASES

Bibliographies of current mapping

The mapping of Latin American countries is uneven in coverage and quality. The one current listing devoted to the area is the biennial "Cartography" section in the "Social sciences" volume of the Handbook of Latin American studies (Gainesville, University of Florida Press). Otherwise there are only the world-wide lists. One of the most useful of these is Geo-Katalog, issued annually by Geo-Center, Internationales Landkartenhaus, Stuttgart. It includes a section on current maps and atlases available for the American continent, arranged alphabetically by country (the entries are in German, English and French). Geo-Center also issues Geo-Kartenbrief, an updated list of maps available, published at irregular intervals and arranged according to a thematic classification.

In the United Kingdom the most recent catalogue of available maps to be published is:

> International maps and atlases in print, editor Kenneth L. Winch, 2.ed. (London & New York, Bowker, 1976) - arranged by the Universal Decimal Classification: sections on Central America and the West Indies are on pp.441-469, and on South America on pp.505-533, followed by accompanying index maps to indicate coverage.

Most Commonwealth countries, and some other developing countries, are covered in:

> Great Britain. Directorate of overseas surveys: Catalogue of maps published by the Directorate of overseas (geodetic and topographical) surveys. (Tolworth, Surrey, the Directorate, 1960) - updated by:

Bibliographies of current mapping (cont'd.)

> Technical co-operation, a monthly bibliography.
> (London, Ministry of Overseas Development
> library, January 1964-   ) - part iv lists map
> additions to the Directorate of overseas surveys.

General atlas

The most recent general atlas devoted to Latin America is
the Atlas Latinskoi Ameriki, published in Moscow in 1968.

Retrospective bibliography

For earlier mapping the most informative catalogue is
A catalogue of maps of Hispanic America including maps in
scientific periodicals ... and sheet and atlas maps ... ,
published by the American Geographical Society of New
York, in 4 vols, 1930-32. More recent is:

> Monteiro, Palmyra V.M.: A catalogue of Latin
> American flat maps 1926-1964.   (Austin,
> Institute of Latin American studies of the Uni-
> versity of Texas, 2 vols, 1967-69) - includes a
> useful introduction to the subject.

A descriptive account (with graphic indexes) of the map
coverage for 19 Central and South American countries is
given in an Annotated index of aerial photographic coverage
and mapping of topography and natural resources, undertaken in the Latin American member countries of the Organization of American States   (Washington, Pan American
Union, 1964-65); for each country a separate collection of
index sheets has been prepared with accompanying text dis-
cussing the aerial photography, topographic mapping, geology, soil, land capability, vegetation and land use surveys
undertaken.

Maps & atlases

Pre-1900

There is no single bibliography of Latin American maps
drawn or published before 1900, although the first volume of
a proposed collection of facsimiles of important older maps
covering South America and its regions was published as
early as 1942:

> Guillén y Tato, Julio Fernando: Monumenta charto-
> graphica indiana. Vol 1: Regiones del Plata y
> Magellánica. (Madrid, 1942).

Discussion of particular maps may be found in works on the
history of cartography and of exploration and in the specialist
journal Imago mundi (Berlin, etc., 1935-   ).

Bibliography of individual countries

Argentina:

> Pusch, Roberto: Catálogo de mapas, planos y croquis
> de la República argentina, y parte de los paises
> limitrofes. (Buenos Aires, Sección de publicacio-
> nes y información del Ministerio de agricultura,
> 1935);

> Turco Greco, Carlos A.: Catálogo cartográfico de la
> República argentina. (Buenos Aires, Editorial
> universitaria de Buenos Aires, for Consejo nacional
> de investigaciones científicas y técnicas, 1967).

Brazil:

> Brazil. Ministerio das relações exteriores.
> Mapoteca: Mapas e planos manuscritos relativos
> ao Brasil colonial conservados no Ministério das
> relações exteriores 1500-1822, descritos por Isa
> Adonias. (Rio de Janeiro, Serviço de documen-
> tação do MRE, 2 vols, 1960);

Maps & atlases

Bibliography of individual countries

Brazil: (cont'd.)

> Brazil. Serviço geográfico do exército: Catálogo
> das cartas e obras diversas, 2.ed. (Rio de
> Janeiro, Diretoria do Serviço, 1959).

These may be supplemented by the irregularly published
Bibliografia cartográfica (formerly ... do Brasil) from the
Mapoteca of the MRE, and by regional works such as the
SUDENE's Bibliografia cartográfica do Nordeste of 1965,
and Isa Adonias's A cartografia da região amazônica ...
1500-1961 (Rio de Janeiro, C.N.P., 2 vols, 1963). Two
important atlases are:

> Brazil. Conselho nacional de geografia: Atlas
> nacional do Brasil, [nova ed.]. (Rio de
> Janeiro, 1966);

> Instituto brasileiro de geografia. Departamento
> de cartografia: Brasil: carta internacional do
> mundo ao milionésimo ... , edição comemorativa
> do sesquicentenário da Independência. (Rio de
> Janeiro, IBG, 1972) - bearing the cover title
> 'Carta do Brasil ao milionésimo'.

Central America:

> Kapp, Kit S.: Central America early maps, up
> to 1860. (North Bend, Ohio, the Author, 1974);

> Palmerlee, Albert E.: Maps of Costa Rica: an
> annotated cartobibliography. (Lawrence,
> University of Kansas Libraries, 1965).

Chile:

> Medina, José Toribio: Ensayo acerca de una
> mapoteca chilena. (Santiago, Ercilla, 1889,
> reprinted 1952).

Bibliography of individual countries (cont'd.)

Colombia:

> Cortes, Vicenta: Catálogo de mapas de Colombia.
> (Madrid, Cultura hispánica, 1967);
>
> Kapp, Kit S.: The early maps of Colombia up to
> 1850 (London, Map Collectors' Circle, 1971).

The Cortes work was too early to include:

> Colombia. Instituto geográfico Agustín Codazzi:
> Atlas de Colombia; planeó ... Eduardo Acevedo
> Latorre, 2.ed. (Bogotá, the Institute, 1969).

Cuba:

> Figarola Caneda, Dimongo: Cartografía cubana del
> British Museum ...: catálogo cronológico de los
> siglos diez y seis al diez y nueva, 2.ed. (Havana,
> Imprensa nacional, 1910);
>
> United States of America. Library of Congress:
> List of books relating to Cuba, by A.P.C.Griffin,
> with a bibliography of maps, by Philip Lee
> Phillips, 2.ed. (Washington, GPO, 1898).

There is also an excellent recent atlas:

> Atlas nacional de Cuba en el décimo aniversario
> de la revolución, elaborado por el Instituto de
> geografía de la Academia de Ciencias de Cuba, y
> el Instituto de geografía de la Academia de Cien-
> cias de la URSS. (Havana, 1970).

Maps & atlases

Bibliography of individual countries   (cont'd.)

Mexico:

> Tamayo, Jorge L., and Alcorta Guerrero, R.:
> Catálogo de la Exposición de Cartografía
> Mexicana.   (Mexico City, Cultura, for Insti-
> tuto panamericano de geografía e historia, 1941);

> Torres Lanzas, Pedro: Relación descriptiva de
> los mapas, planos & [sic] de Mexico y Florida
> existentes en el Archivo general de Indias.
> (Seville, El Mercantil, 2 vols, 1900).

Panama:

> Canal Zone Library-Museum, Balboa Heights:
> Subject catalog of the special Panama collec-
> tion of the Canal Zone Library-Museum.
> (Boston, Mass., Hall, 1964);

> Kapp, Kit S.: The early maps of Panama up to
> 1865.   (London, Map Collectors' Circle, 1971).

The national atlas is:

> Atlas de Panamá.   (Panama City, Comisión del
> Atlas, 1965).

Peru:

> Temple, Ella Dunbar: "La cartografía peruana
> actual, con particular referencia a los últimos
> planos de desarrollo nacional", Boletín de la
> Sociedad geográfica de Lima, 1964, and as off-
> print, Departamento de geografía de la Univer-
> sidad Nacional de San Marcos, 1965?

- which was too early to include:

> Atlas histórico, geográfico y de paisajes peru-
> anos.   (Lima, Instituto nacional de planeación,
> 1969).

Bibliography of individual countries   (cont'd.)

Surinam:

> Koeman, Cornelis: Bibliography of printed maps of Suriname 1671-1971.   (Amsterdam, Theatrum Orbis Terrarum, 1973);
>
> Koeman, Cornelis: Land- en zeekarten van Suriname. Schakels met het verleden. (Amsterdam, 1973).

Venezuela:

> Spain. Archivo general de Indias, Seville: Mapas, planos y dibujos sobre Venezuela existentes en el Archivo general de Indias, por F. Morales Padrón y J. Llavador Mira.   (Seville, 1964-   ).

West Indies and Commonwealth countries:

The early maps of many Commonwealth territories have been listed by the Map Collectors' Circle. For instance:

> Kapp, Kit S.: The printed maps of Jamaica up to 1825.   (London, Map Collectors' Circle, 1968);
>
> Map Collectors' Circle: Some early printed maps of Trinidad and Tobago ... (London, Map Collectors' Circle, 1964).

A bibliography of recent maps is:

> Lall, Kissoon O.M.: Mapping in Guyana since 1940: a review and its relevance to national development. (Georgetown, Department of Geography of the University of Guyana, 1975) - appendix ii (pages 79-81) lists maps and plans by the Cartographic Division of the Lands Department.

Bibliography of individual countries

West Indies and Commonwealth countries: (cont'd.)

A recent atlas is:

> Atlas of the Commonwealth of the Bahamas.
> (Kingston, Jamaica, Kingston Publishers, for
> the Ministry of Education of the Bahamas,
> 1976).

Map collections in the United Kingdom

Most universities teaching Latin American studies have col-
lections of maps and atlases of the region, either in the university library or in the university's geography department.
In London there is a collection in University College Library,
and in the Canning House Library of the Hispanic & Luso-
Brazilian Council, whilst the Institute of Latin American
Studies Library has built up a collection of Latin American
town plans. Other collections can be discovered from
Naylor's Directory of libraries and special collections on
Latin America and the West Indies   (Athlone Press, 1975) -
consult the index under 'maps'.

There is also a World directory of map collections, edited
by Walter W. Ristow, and published in 1976 by the International Federation of Library Associations (IFLA) - pages
237-264 cover the U.K.

The major general map collections in central London that
have good coverage of the region are:

> British Library Reference Division Department
> of Manuscripts - includes pre-1900 maps of
> Latin America; has published: Manuscript maps,
> charts and plans and topographical drawings in
> the British Museum, 3 vols, 1844-61;

Maps & atlases

Map collections in the United Kingdom   (cont'd.)

British Library Reference Division Map Library -
a copyright deposit library (i.e. receives a copy
of all maps published in the British Isles); also
includes a large collection of earlier Latin American maps, as well as many foreign and modern
surveys. Its Catalogue of printed maps, charts
and plans, 15 vols, published 1967; supplement
1965-1974 published 1978.

Public Record Office - published: Maps and plans
in the Public Record Office, Vol 2: America and
the West Indies, 1974;

Royal Geographical Society - worldwide coverage.
Publishes six-monthly accessions list: New geographical literature and maps.

At Greenwich there is:

The National Maritime Museum Library - particularly important for West Indian material. Consult
its Catalogue of the library, Vol 3: Atlases and
cartography   (HMSO, 2 parts, 1971).

Outside London there are three copyright deposit libraries
aiming at worldwide coverage:

Cambridge University Library Map Room;

National Library of Scotland (Edinburgh) Map Room;

Oxford University Bodleian Library Map Section -
issues a monthly select accessions list.

[ST]

MICROFORM MATERIAL

Format

'Microform' and 'microtext' are generic terms to cover all
types of document reproduction by microphotography. Although roll microfilms (reels of 35 mm transparencies) are
by far the commonest form, there are several others:
microfiches (transparencies the size of library catalogue
cards, particularly favoured in continental Europe), micro-
cards (similar in size, but opaque) and microprints (also
opaque, but larger). Consequent differences in reading
equipment and storage arrangements may result in different
procedures in the library for their access and use. They
may be recorded in a separate catalogue or catalogues, and,
even if included in the main author catalogue, may be omitted from the subject catalogue.

Types of material in microtext

The original purpose of microform was to save storage
space, whence it was used for such things as back-runs of
newspapers and other bulky material. Its cheapness has
since made it a convenient way of copying anything; this
means in effect that your library may hold in microfilm, etc.
practically any item it has been unable, for any reason, to
obtain in the original.

There is also a certain amount of material which has its
original publication in microform: for instance the
Catalogue of the Amsterdam Centrum voor studie en doku-
menatie van Latijns America ('CEDLA'), which is a quarterly accessions list of all Latin American material added
to Dutch university libraries.

Bibliography

Since any institution (or individual) may reproduce something in microform, for its (or his) own use or limited distribution, no one can ever list everything available in this
format. Commercially published microforms on Latin
America were listed in:

Microform material

Bibliography (cont'd.)

Diaz, Albert J.: "Selected list of microreproduced material relating to Latin America", Ninth Seminar on the Acquisition of Latin American Library Materials (SALALM), St.Louis, 1964 (Working paper 6).

Subsequent SALALM's have been supplementing this with an annual "Microfilming projects newsletter", which also reports on non-commercial projects.

Microfilmed archives

Microreproduction is perhaps most important in making archive material more widely available. The few sporadic indexes to this material have been sponsored by well-financed organisations with international cultural responsibilities. The Instituto panamericano de geografía e historia's typescript Guía de los documentos microfotografia-dos por la Unidad móvil de microfilm de la UNESCO of 1963 covered material from Peru, Paraguay, Panama, El Salvador and the Dominican Republic, and in 1960 the Fundación John Boulton published an index to the collection of microfilms prepared by it on the history of Venezuela 1810-1830. Diplomatic, political, economic and social material from the Department of State archives relating to Latin American countries since the early nineteenth-century has been made available by the United States National Archives and Records Service in its latest Catalog of National Archives microfilm publications.

A general listing of material available in North America is:

Hale, Richard W.: Guide to photocopied historical materials in the United States and Canada. (Ithaca, NY, Cornell University Press for the American Historical Association, 1961).

Microform material

Microfilmed archives (cont'd.)

Microfilming of the archives of the countries of the Caribbean formed a subject of ACURIL IX (the ninth conference
of the Association of Caribbean university, research and
institutional libraries) at Wilemstad, Curaçao in November
1977 - see the Library of Congress information bulletin,
36(50), Dec. 16 1977, pp.823-830.

Newspapers on microfilm

See the concluding paragraphs of 'Tracking down the title
you want' in our section 'NEWS & CURRENT AFFAIRS -
NEWSPAPERS'.

[LH, RP]

MUSIC

Bibliography

Recent, but very brief (37 mimeographed pages) is:

> Casa de las Américas, Havana: Bibliografía de
> música latinoamericana. (Havana, the Casa,
> 1972) - based on holdings of the Casa itself, the
> Cuban National Library and the library of Havana
> University.

Much more extensive (411 pages) but now 15 years out of
date is:

> Chase, Gilbert: A guide to the music of Latin
> America, 2.ed. (Washington, Pan American
> Union, 1962, reprinted New York, AMS Press,
> 1972) - by country: under each, the unrevised
> text of the first (1945) edition is followed by a
> lengthy supplement.

A rather specialised work too recent for inclusion in the
above is:

> Davis, Martha E.: Music and dance in Latin
> American urban contexts: a selective biblio-
> graphy. (Brockport?, NY, the author?, 1973).

Space precludes an extensive listing of guides to the music
of individual countries, but we give an example of one to the
music of Brazil, probably the country with the most extensive musical literature in the region:

> Azevedo, Luis Heitor Correia de, and others:
> Bibliografia musical brasileira 1820-1950.
> (Rio de Janeiro, Instituto nacional do livro,
> 1952) - briefly annotated references to both
> books and periodical articles.

Music

Biographical information

The standard source for bio-bibliographical information on Latin American composers is the multi-volume Composi-tores de América: datos biográficos y catálogos de sus obras, begun in 1955 by the Music division (later the Division of music and visual arts) of the Pan American Union (since 1970 the General secretariat of the Organization of American States), and still in progress.

On a much smaller scale there are:

Cardoso, Silvio Tito: Dicionário biográfico de música popular. (Rio de Janeiro, 1965) - and:

Mariz, Vasco: Dicionário bio-bibliográfico musical, brasileiro e internacional. (Rio de Janeiro, Kosmos, 1948).

Book Reviews

New books and periodicals are reviewed in the Organization of American States' Boletín inter-americano de música. Prior to September 1957 this formed part of the Pan American Union's Boletín de música y artes visuales (March 1950-June 1956).

There is also a regular section on music in the two-yearly "Humanities" volume of the Handbook of Latin American Studies (published by the University of Florida at Gainesville for the Library of Congress Latin American, Portuguese and Spanish Division).

Music

Periodical indexes

Music index (Detroit, Information services, monthly,
1949-   ) appears promptly and has good coverage of
Latin American music. The annual Bibliographie des
Musickschrifttums (Frankfurt a.M., Hofmeister, now
Mainz, Schott, 1936-   )provides country references in
its catchword index, but has a four years timelag.

Libraries

British libraries with appreciable collections of Latin
American music include Westminster Central Music Lib-
rary (Buckingham Palace Road), the Library of the British
Institute of Recorded Sound (Exhibition Road, London SW7),
the Library of the University of London at Senate House
(Malet Street, London WC1) and Canning House Library of
the Hispanic and Luso-Brazilian Council (Belgrave Square,
London SW1).

There are large North American collections in Washington,
at the Columbus Memorial Library of the O.A.S. and the
Library of Congress, in Minneapolis, at the Library of the
University of Minnesota, and in the Lilley Library on the
Bloomington campus of the University of Indiana.

Library catalogues

An important recent published catalogue is:

> Indiana University. School of Music. Latin
> American Music Center: Music from Latin
> America available at Indiana University:
> scores, tapes and records, 2.ed., compiled
> by Juan Orrego Salas. (Bloomington, Ind.,
> The Center, 1971).

Recorded music

see the section 'AUDIO-VISUAL MATERIAL'.

[LH]

NATIONAL BIBLIOGRAPHY

Books about the individual countries

A list of the principal guides to works about the individual countries of Spanish America and Brazil is provided on pages 650-651 of:

> Encyclopedia of Latin America, edited by Helen Delpar. (New York, McGraw Hill, 1974).

For the West Indies and the Guianas there is:

> Comitas, Lambros: Caribbeana,1900-1965: a topical bibliography. (Seattle, University of Washington Press, 1968).

Books published in the individual countries - current

Practically every country in the Americas has made efforts to produce a current national register of its book and serial production, usually as an annual, but sometimes as a quarterly or even monthly publication. Some of these began in the last century; others, such as those of the newly independent Commonwealth countries, are quite recent. Unfortunately, in almost every case, limited funds, insufficient staff, and the lack of effective laws compelling publishers to deposit copies of their output with the national library (or other bibliographic centre) have prevented these attempts from being really comprehensive - or even prompt and regular in appearance.

The position as it was in 1970 is well described in:

> Zimmerman, Irene: Current national bibliographies of Latin America. (Gainesville, University of Florida, 1971),

and this may be updated by reference to the brief survey (pp.141-143) in:

National bibliography

(cont'd.)

> Naylor, Bernard: "A comprehensive loan collec-
> tion of Latin American material", in, Ligue des
> bibliothèques européennes de recherche: Acqui-
> sitions from the Third World: papers of the
> LIBER seminar 17-19 September 1973, edited
> by Derek A. Clarke.   (London, Mansell, 1975),

and for the Commonwealth Caribbean countries, by reference to:

> Commonwealth Secretariat: Commonwealth
> national bibliographies: an annotated direc-
> tory, compiled by Susan Kennedy and others.
> (London, Publications section of the Secre-
> tariat, 1977).

The cases of Cuba, Chile and Brazil are treated in greater
detail in:

> International conference on Cuban acquisition and
> bibliography, Library of Congress, Washington,
> 1970: Cuban acquisitions and bibliography, pro-
> ceedings and working papers ... , edited by Earl
> J. Pariseau.   (Washington, Hispanic Foundation
> of the Library of Congress, 1970);

> Freudenthal, Juan R.: "Chilean national biblio-
> graphy, origins and progress", Libri 22(4),
> Oct. 1972, pp.273-280;

> Hallewell, Laurence: "The development of
> national bibliography in Brazil", Libri 23(4),
> Oct. 1973, pp.291-297.

For recent developments see the section "Bibliographic
services throughout the world" in UNESCO's Bibliography,
documentation, terminology (Paris, alternate months).
Articles on the national bibliographic services of each U.N.

National bibliography

<u>Books published in the individual countries - current</u>
(cont'd.)

member country appear at irregular intervals, to update
the information originally given in P. Avicenne's <u>Biblio-
graphic services</u> throughout the world, 1965-1969.

Copies of Latin American and West Indian national bibliographies held in British & Irish libraries may be traced
through:

> Committee on Latin America: <u>Latin American
> serials</u>, volume 3: <u>Literature with language,
> art and music</u>, edited by L. Hallewell.   (London,
> COLA,
>   1977).

Booksellers' catalogues

Often the most practical way to keep up with current Latin
American book and periodical production is through the
perusal of booksellers' catalogues. Most firms interested
in selling to libraries and individuals in this country (including all those listed in our section "BOOKSELLERS")
produce regular lists, in some cases every month. Naturally their readiness to supply these depends on the size
and frequency of the orders they receive in return. One of
the best, <u>Livros novos</u> from J. Heydecker of Atlantis
Livros of São Paulo, which aims to cover all new Brazilian
publications, is normally available only on subscription.

International publications

For sources covering more than one country, see the
section 'Bibliographies - Hispanic language material'.

Retrospective bibliographies

Bibliographers in a couple of the smaller countries have
attempted a complete listing of books published in them, or
about them: Miguel A. García for Honduras (where printing

Retrospective bibliographies (cont'd.)

began in 1620) and Carlos F. S. Fernández Caballero for Paraguay (where it began in 1724).

The indefatigable José Toribio Medina was responsible for a vast series of works covering colonial and early nineteenth-century printing in a number of Latin American cities, from Mexico City to Santiago de Chile.

Brazil had no real indigenous printing before 1808, but books by Brazilians and books about Brazil published outside the country have been recorded in Rubens Borba de Moraes's Bibliografia brasileira do período colonial (São Paulo, USP, 1969).

For Venezuela there is currently in progress (but limited to 'obras de literatura, historia y de índole general'):

> Villasana, Ángel Raúl: Ensayo de un repertorio bibliográfico venezolano. (Caracas, Banco Central de Venezuela, 1969-   ) - an author catalogue.

Other sources

For many purposes, a convenient substitute for national bibliographies, both current and retrospective, is provided by the published catalogues of various libraries with important Latin American collections. These are discussed in our section 'PUBLISHED CATALOGUES'. The most important of them for current material is the United States National Union Catalog. Since Latin American works do not usually appear in it until a year or two after publication, it is worth noting that there exists a special advance list of Brazilian titles, the Library of Congress accessions list, Brazil (alternate months from January 1975), issued by the Library of Congress Office in Rio de Janeiro. The bimonthly issues exclude periodicals, which are recorded in a special number at the end of each year.

[LH]

Latin American newspapers

Newspapers are unique and invaluable sources of information and opinion. They are also expensive, bulky and fragile - which makes libraries reluctant to acquire or keep them.

The best collections of Latin American newspapers in this country are at the British Library's Newspaper Library (at Colindale in North London), at Saint Antony's College, Oxford, and at the University of Essex. A collection is also being built up by the CONTEMPORARY ARCHIVE ON LATIN AMERICA (q.v.). The West India Committee Library (now housed at the Library of the University of London Institute of Commonwealth Studies) has a useful collection within its area of interest.

None of these sources can provide a very up-to-date service, as they have seamail subscriptions, or take quarterly microfilm copy. For the most recent issues you may find it worthwhile enquiring at embassies and consulates, who will almost certainly receive their countries' major newspapers airmail.

North American newspaper collections are listed in:

> Parch, Grace D., ed.: <u>Directory of newspaper libraries in the U.S. and Canada.</u>   (New York, Special Libraries Association, 1976).

A universal problem, but one that is particularly important in Latin America, is that of discovering how much (and in what direction) newspapers are influenced by governmental and other external pressures. The student should always be on his guard against sudden changes in these factors. Beware of interpreting a newspaper's current content solely in the light of its past policies.

News & current affairs - newspapers

Foreign newspapers

European and North American papers are received more promptly and are available in many more libraries, but only a few are notable for their coverage of Latin America. Le Monde, the New York Times, the Neue Zürcher Zeitung are examples. Coverage in U.K. newspapers is not so good, but the Times and the Financial Times will be found useful.

Tracking down the title you want

There is no up-to-date list of newspapers of Latin American interest in U.K. libraries. A mimeographed sheet with locations was issued some years ago by the London Institute of Latin American Studies, but this is now outdated. The Social Science Research Council has recently produced:

> Webber, Rosemary: World list of national newspapers: a union list of national newspapers in libraries in the British Isles.   (London, Butterworths, 1976).

This excludes the holdings of the British Library's Newspaper Library (which has just published its own catalogue), but it also has many other omissions: El Día, Excelsior, Heraldo de México and Nacional (all held by libraries in this country) are examples of its omissions from Mexico alone. Among its entries for Brazil, we note the absence of the Estado de São Paulo.

Enquiry of the BRITISH UNION CATALOGUE OF LATIN AMERICANA (q.v.) should therefore supplement use of Webber, but even this is probably incomplete, and you should also contact likely libraries direct.

It is not feasible to borrow 'hard copy' of newspapers through inter-library loan, but it is worth trying for photocopies of articles - if your details are precise enough.

Tracking down the title you want (cont'd.)

Remember that page number is seldom sufficient: most papers are North American in style and size, with many sections (numbered or lettered), each with its own pagination.

The Foreign Newspapers Project of the (American) Association of Research Libraries has built up in Chicago a large microfilm archive of Latin American (and other) newspapers, which it lends to members. This service is not available through normal international inter-library loan, but if the demand in your institution justifies it, you may want to persuade your library to take out a direct membership of the scheme.

The United States Library of Congress and the Biblioteca nacional in Rio de Janeiro have a joint project for microfilming Brazilian newspapers. This is providing both libraries with complete microfilm copies of O Estado de São Paulo (from 1875) and O Jornal do Commercio (from 1827), and eventually (we presume) of other titles too.

Bibliographies

Current publications are well covered in:

> Feuereisen, Fritz, and Schmacke, E.: Die Presse in Lateinamerika, ein Handbuch für Wirtschaft und Werbung. (Pullach-München, Dokumentation, 1968, 2.ed., 1973).

There is also a list of dailies in:

> Chilcote, Ronald H.: The press in Latin America, Spain and Portugal, a summary of recent developments. (Palo Alto, Institute of Hispanic American and Luso-Brazilian Studies of Stanford University, 1963).

Bibliographies (cont'd.)

Nearly 6,000 titles held by American libraries - including many long since defunct - are listed in:

> Charno, Steven M.: Latin American newspapers in United States libraries, a union list. (Austin, University of Texas Press, 1968).

Older material is covered in:

> United States of America. Library of Congress: A chronological listing of leading Latin American newspapers, by John L. Hardesty. (Washington, GPO, 1965).

Newspapers omitted from Charno and Hardesty (because they are held by no U.S. library) are partially recorded in:

> Gutiérrez Witt, Laura: "Newspaper titles from Colombia, Ecuador and Venezuela unavailable in U.S. libraries, a survey", Eighteenth Seminar on the Acquisition of Latin American Library Materials, Port of Spain, 1973 (Working paper C-1).

A bibliography of works about the press is:

> Gardner, Mary A.: The press of Latin America, a tentative and selective bibliography in Spanish and Portuguese. (Austin, University of Texas Press, 1973).

Indexes

Unless the precise date of an event is known, newspapers can be very tedious to use in research, for very few are indexed. There are indexes to a few recent years of the Caracas papers Nacional and Universal, and the Instituto de investigaciones históricas of the Universidad de la República in Montevideo has done a small amount of indexing of newspaper articles on Uruguayan history (its Fichas

Indexes (cont'd.)

correspondientes al año 1958 appeared in 1961). Also, several Mexican newspapers of last century have been indexed in the series "Periódicos y escritores del siglo diez y nueve" which the Boletín bibliográfico de la Secretaría de hacienda y crédito público [de los Estados Unidos Mexicanos] has been including since June 1966; during 1973 the same journal published an index also to the Gazeta de Mexico of 1784. In Jamaica the Gleaner is currently being indexed by the West India Reference Library.

Fortunately the thrice-monthly index to the New York Times (from 1912, but being extended back in time) - cumulated annually - can often serve to fix the date of an event, which may then be easily traced elsewhere. There is also a single-volume Obituaries index to the paper covering 1858-1968.

The similar Official index to the London Times is monthly, with quarterly cumulations. It began in 1906, and since January 1973 has also covered the Times literary supplement, the Times educational supplement, the Times higher education supplement and the Sunday Times (although hardly any libraries acquire Sunday papers). For the period before the Official index there is Palmer's index to the "Times" newspaper, 1790-1941, and also an index to the paper's references to Brazil, in:

> Graham, Richard, and Valiela, V.: Brazil in the London "Times" 1850-1905. (Carbondale, SALALM, 1969).

If you are doing research on North America you might be helped by:

> Miller, Anita C.: Newspaper indexes: a location and subject guide for researchers. (Metuchen, Scarecrow, 1977).

Clippings

Even better than an index is a subject-arranged collection of newspaper cuttings, but few libraries can afford the staff to maintain one. The Economics Department Library of Lloyds Bank International (formerly the Bank of London & South America) and Chatham House Library (at the Royal Institute of International Affairs) both have such collections going back to the 1920's, although the Chatham House one is limited to material on the region appearing in European papers. There is also a collection of press cuttings mainly from European and North American sources at the CONTEMPOR-ARY ARCHIVE ON LATIN AMERICA (q.v.). A very detailed "Presse Archiv" (three-quarters from Latin American sources) is maintained by the Institut für Iberoamerika-Kunde of Hamburg: this was begun some ten years ago.

Information Services on Latin America, of Berkeley, Ca., publishes ISLA, a monthly service of reproductions of clippings from leading U.S. newspapers (including the Manchester Guardian-Le Monde weekly North American edition), with a six-monthly index. This began in July 1970. Although it is unfortunately regarded as too expensive by many British libraries, a current copy is taken by the University of London Library (at Senate House, Malet Street) who pass the outdated copies for permanent filing at the British Library Reference Division in the British Museum.

CIDOC

By way of postscript, we should like to draw your attention to the publications of the recently defunct Centro intercultural de documentación (CIDOC) of Cuernavaca, Mexico. Most of these were collections of press cuttings from Latin American newspapers, on particular subjects: ranging from Venezuelan tax reform or the birth-control controversy in Brazil, to how the continent's press reacted to the death of Ernesto Guevara. The variety of newspapers so covered is considerably greater than those to which the U.K. library user will normally have access.

CIDOC (cont'd.)

There is a complete collection of CIDOC publications held by the British Library Reference Division and a partial collection at the University of Essex Library.

[LH]

NEWS & CURRENT AFFAIRS -
OTHER SOURCES

News digests

Information latine of Paris and Agencia Efe of Madrid are
daily; the former began in 1949. Facts on file (from 1944)
and Deadline data on world affairs (a card service begun in
1955) are American weekly digests with worldwide coverage.
Keesing's contemporary archives, also weekly and world-
wide, is Dutch in origin, but its U.K. edition (started in
1931) is the most widely subscribed digest in British libraries; unfortunately its scope is restricted by concentration on
formal, legal events, such as government changes, election
results and international agreements (given in textual detail).

Latin America Newsletters of London issue three weekly digests that, although brief, are not afraid to express opinions:
Latin America political report (prior to 1977, just Latin
America), begun in April 1967, Latin America economic
report (from 1973), and, most recent, Latin America com-
modities report. Their very brevity does mean a low price
(with special rates for individuals) and you should seriously
consider having your own personal subscription to the LAPR.

American digests devoted exclusively to Latin American
affairs range from the leftist North American Congress on
Latin America (NACLA)'s Latin America and empire report
(monthly from 1966) to the businessman's Hanson's Latin
American letter (Washington, weekly from 1945). There is
the very journalistic Times of the Americas (Washington,
weekly from 1957) and the brief quarterly Latin American
digest of Arizona State University's Center for Latin American Studies (from 1966). For the period 1948-1964 you can
also consult the defunct monthly Hispanic American report
from Stanford University. Two recent additions (both from
1973) are the Latin American index (Washington, Latin
American Research, fortnightly) and the Latin American
report: an independent digest of political and economic events
(San Francisco, World Affairs Council of Northern California).

145

News & current affairs - other sources

News digests (cont'd.)

Cuba produces the bi-monthly Prensa latina (published in
Mexico City),and economic news items are noted in the
monthly Archivo de prensa of the Servicio de información
y biblioteca of the Instituto para la integración de América
latina (a Buenos Aires subsidiary of the Inter-American
Development Bank), which began in 1973. From the Instituto
de cultura hispánica in Madrid comes the Resumen mensual
(from 1971).

Annual surveys

The Resúmenes mensuales are also published in annual
volumes called Sintesis informativa iberoamericana, which
seem to have replaced the earlier Anuario iberoamericano
(1962-1969). The Madrid Institute also issues Documentación iberoamericana: crónica de un año, rather after the
style of Keesing's contemporary archives, with full texts of
important documents and full indexes; this began with the
volume for 1963 but has fallen increasingly into publication
arrears: 1969 is still awaited.

More up-to-date is the very brief Latin American yearly
review from the American College in Paris, which started
with the survey of 1973. There are also the supplements to
one or two Latin American encyclopaedias issued as 'books
of the year', e.g. the Anuários of the Enciclopédia BARSA
of Rio de Janeiro, and the publishers of Facts on file also
produce an annual on Latin America.

Data banks

The New York Times provides an abstracting service to
current affairs in machine-readable form, the New York
Times information bank: see the section 'DATA BANKS &
INFORMATION IN MACHINE READABLE FORMAT'.

News & current affairs - other sources

News magazines

The Time/Newsweek formula has been imitated in practically every country of the Americas. Examples are Tiempo
of Mexico City, Veja and Visão of São Paulo, Ercilla of
Santiago de Chile. Titles and holdings of such periodicals in
British and Irish libraries will be found in:

> Committee on Latin America: Latin American
> history with politics, a serials list. (London,
> Gregg International, 1973).

Broadcasting

The BBC Monitoring service provides information on
foreign broadcasting in two publications: its daily Monitoring report and its six-times weekly Summary of world
broadcasting (of which Part 5 covers 'Latin America and
other countries').

Bibliography

News digests, newsletters, news bulletins and news sources
and agencies are listed in:

> Vivó, Paquita: Latin America, a selected list
> of sources. (Washington, The Latin American
> Service, 1972).

[LH]

OFFICIAL PUBLICATIONS

Official publications - 'government documents' as Americans call them - originate at every level of government: municipal, provincial, national and international. For dependent territories there will also be relevant publishing by the metropolitan authorities.

They can be important in almost every field of study, from pure science to literature. This is particularly the case in the smaller Latin American countries that lack any significant commercial book industry. In the case of the West Indies there is a useful introduction to the range and nature of government publishing:

> Hallewell, Laurence: "West Indian official publishing, and U.K. official publishing on the West Indies ...", Twenty-first Seminar on the Acquisition of Latin American Library Materials, Bloomington (Ind.), 1976, (Working paper B-10).

Unfortunately, official publishing presents its own special difficulties, both in discovering what has been published, and in locating a known item in a library catalogue. Authorship is occasionally attributed to a named individual, but this is exceptional, and usually ignored by library catalogues. Most libraries enter all government publications under the name of the Country, or other political unit, with the name of the department immediately responsible as a sub-heading. Some libraries, however, use other systems: e.g. Political unit. Date. Title; or, Political unit. Ministry. Department. Title. Sometimes, if the publishing organisation is deemed sufficiently autonomous, its name may be made the 'entry word' with no reference to the country or other political unit under which it functions (e.g. Fundação Getúlio Vargas; or, Instituto brasileiro de geografia). Some libraries may even enter official publications directly under the title of each work. A frequent convention is to index official pronouncements by presidents, governors and other

Citation (cont'd.)

office holders under the political unit, with the name of
their office as a sub-heading; this applies to such things as
state of the nation messages to the legislature. Thus:

> PARAIBA. Governador, 1966-70 (João Agripino
> Filho)   Mensagem ao poder legislativo,
>   1969.

Periodicals and serials are usually entered under title, but
many catalogues enter them under the issuing department
(itself under the country etc.) - particularly when the title
is not distinctive ('Boletín de ...', 'Anuario do ...' etc.).
They may be found in a separate catalogue, or they may be
filed among the monographs.

You can also be misled by the form of name used in the
heading. 'Great Britain', for instance, is more usual than
'United Kingdom', but the British Museum General catalogue of books prefers 'England'. Most American catalogues have 'Argentine republic' rather than 'Argentina'
and 'Catholic Church' instead of 'Roman Catholic Church'.
Older libraries may perpetuate earlier spellings: 'Bello
Horizonte', 'Hayti', 'Parahyba' etc.

Inversion of headings to favour the most significant word,
e.g. 'Trinidad. Education and culture, Ministry of' may be
met with, but is nowadays less common than the direct
form, 'Trinidad. Ministry of education and culture'.

Different libraries also cope in different ways with the
habit official bodies have of constantly changing their
names, and the names, style and periodicity of their publications. Material appearing at well-spaced intervals -
five-year plans, for instance - is particularly liable to
"change hands" between one publication and the next. Library catalogues vary a great deal in the amount of detailed
cross-referencing they make between successive names of
government organisations, but the United States National

Citation (cont'd.)

Union Catalog (discussed under 'PRINTED CATALOGUES')
will be found particularly helpful in this respect.

Another problem, affecting us all in the modern world, but
particularly troublesome in Latin America, is the bureau-
cracy's love of acronyms. Some suggestions to help you
trace the full form (almost invariably the cataloguer's preference) are made under 'ABBREVIATIONS AND ACRO-
NYMS'.

Before beginning a search for any official publication, make
sure you know your library's cataloguing practice. If the
library guide is not explicit, get the library staff to explain
it to you.

Bibliographies - general

The searcher will often find he lacks sufficient details to
track down an item in his library's catalogue. When this happens, or when there is a need to know what government publications have been issued on a certain topic, there are a number of guides that may be consulted.

The most recent comprehensive guide, in which 17 pages are
devoted to Latin America, is:

> Childs, James B.: "Government publications (docu-
> ments)", in Encyclopedia of library and information
> science, vol. 10. (New York, Dekker, 1973), pp.36-
> 140 - also available as a separate publication,
> Washington, Library of Congress, 1973.

Bibliographies - HMSO publications

U.K. official publishing on the area and the relevant guides to
it are outlined in the article by Hallewell under 'Citation'
above. HMSO publications since January 1950 can also be
traced through the British National Bibliography (see:

Bibliographies - HMSO publications (cont'd.)

'PRINTED CATALOGUES'), and HMSO material relating to Trinidad has been listed by:

> McDowell, Wilhelmina: Official publications on Trinidad and Tobago, 1797-1962. (London, Library Association, unpublished Fellowship thesis, Sep. 1971).

Bibliographies - U.S. government publications

> Apperson, Frances, and Cravens, Sally: "U.S. government publications on Latin America", Nineteenth Seminar on the Acquisition of Latin American Library Materials, Austin, Tex., 1974. (Working paper D-7: pp.389-399 of vol.2 of the Final report ...).

Bibliographies - Latin American government publications

No Latin American government issues catalogues of its publications as comprehensive as those of HMSO or of the Government Printing Office (GPO) in Washington, but many individual departments issue lists of their own publishing.

The standard general guide, now rather out-dated, is:

> United States of America. Library of Congress: A guide to the official publications of the other American republics; J.B. Childs, general editor. (Washington, GPO, 19 parts - one for each country except Mexico, covered by Ker's work below -, 1945-49, reprinted in 2 vols, New York, Johnson, 1964) - entries are from the Library of Congress catalogue, arranged under the agencies responsible, with a title index.

The working papers of the annual Seminars on the Acquisition of Latin American Library Materials (SALALM) should also be consulted, particularly Seminars IX, X and

Official publications

Bibliographies - Latin American government publications
(cont'd.)

XI of 1964 to 1966, where there are several lists of official publications. SALALM VIII (1963) includes Fermín Peraza's "Bibliografías sobre publicaciones oficiales de la América latina" (working paper 11), revised and reprinted by the author the following year (Gainesville, 1964).

The various annual national bibliographies (see: 'NATIONAL BIBLIOGRAPHY') also cover official publishing to some degree, and are particularly useful for provincial and local government publications, omitted from most other sources; unfortunately Latin American national bibliographies seldom come out on time, and are sometimes several years behind schedule.

Many research institutes list official publications in their fields of interest, and there are also bibliographies issued by international organisations, such as the UNESCO Bibliographical handbook series.

Organisation manuals are useful since the list of departments gives some indication of the kinds of publications that might be available, and because the exact name of a department is one of the most important but elusive details needed to locate a publication. For these see:

> Mesa, Rosa Quintero: "Bibliography of organization manuals and other sources of information on the governmental organization of the countries of Latin America", Fifteenth Seminar on the Acquisition of Latin American Library Materials, Toronto, 1970, (Working paper 16).

Where manuals are lacking, recent lists of government departments may be found in such publications as the national budgets and national telephone directories (see: 'DIRECTORIES').

Official publications

<u>Bibliographies - Latin American official serials</u>

Since a very large proportion of government publications appear as serials, many can be traced from:

> <u>List of the serial publications of foreign governments 1815-1931</u>, edited by Winifred Gregory [Gould]. (New York, Wilson, 1932) - gives locations in U.S. libraries.

The Gregory list is being superseded, except for Puerto Rico and the Commonwealth Caribbean by:

> Mesa, Rosa Quintero, ed.: <u>Latin American serial documents, a holdings list.</u> (Ann Arbor, University Microfilms, for Florida University Libraries, 1968-   ) - in progress, one volume per country; the most recent have been issued by Bowker of New York. Serials of quasi-official institutions, such as public universities, are included.

<u>Bibliographies - individual countries</u>

Space precludes our listing works on each Latin American country, but we must mention the excellent bibliographies that have appeared for Mexico:

> Ker, Annita M.: <u>Mexican government publications, a guide to the more important publications of the national government of Mexico 1821-1936.</u> (Washington, GPO, 1940) - continued by:

> Fernández Esquivel, Rosa M.: <u>Las publicaciones oficiales de México, guía de publicaciones periódicas y seriadas 1937-1967.</u> (Mexico City, Seminario de investigaciones bibliotecológicas de la UNAM, 1967);

Bibliographies - individual countries (cont'd.)

- and for Brazil:

> Lombardi, Mary: Brazilian serial documents,
> a selected and annotated guide. (Bloomington,
> Ind., Indiana University Press, 1974);

> Richardson, Ivan L.: Bibliografia brasileira de
> administração pública e assuntos correlatos.
> (Rio de Janeiro, Servico de publicações da
> Fundação Getúlio Vargas, 1964).

Bibliographies - Commonwealth countries

Official publications of Commonwealth countries received by
the libraries of the Foreign and Commonwealth Office and of
the Ministry of Overseas Development are recorded in:

> Technical co-operation, a monthly bibliography.
> (London, Ministry of Overseas Development
> Library, Jan.1964-   ).

See also the article "West Indian official publishing" cited
at the head of this section. Not mentioned in Hallewell's
article is the recent comprehensive bibliography (laws and
parliamentary proceedings excepted) of the British Virgin
Islands:

> Penn, Verna E.: Government reports: a union
> catalogue of government reports held in the
> public library and government departments.
> (Tortola, Chief Minister's Office, 1975).

International organisations

The publications of inter-governmental and other international organisations are extremely important in the Latin
American field. One problem in dealing with them is that of
language. Thus it may not be immediately apparent that
your reference to 'CEPAL: Lista de siglas latinoameri-
canas' is met by a library catalogue entry for 'Economic

International organisations (cont'd.)

Commission for Latin America: Latin American initialisms and acronyms'. Also, although publication in two or more languages is almost a rule, it not infrequently happens that the original language edition (whichever that may be) has a fuller text than the translation(s).

The difficulties of locating official publications in library catalogues apply particularly to the output of international organisations. The chief problems, apart from language, are the pervasiveness of acronyms (already mentioned) and the extent to which the library's chosen heading reflects the hierarchy of subordinate bodies and departments; e.g. whether 'Economic Commission for Latin America' be used as a heading in its own right or as a sub-heading under 'United Nations'.

Even among official organisations, the O.A.S. must hold some sort of record for the frequency with which changes are made in the names and functions of its departments and divisions. In particular, you should be aware that what is now its General secretariat was until 1970 the 'Pan American Union', which is treated in most library catalogues as a totally independent body.

"Publications of inter-American and international organizations" is the title of working paper C-2 of the XIX SALALM (Austin, Texas, 1974), which includes:

> Mesa, Rosa Quintero: "The publications of the Inter-American Development Bank", Nineteenth Seminar on the Acquisition of Latin American Library Materials, Austin, 1974, (working paper C-2A: pp.225-237 of vol 2 of the Final report).

Two recent, more general, guides to the publications of international organisations are:

Official publications

International organisations (cont'd.)

> Dimitrov, Théodore Delchev: Documents of international organisations: a bibliographic handbook ... (London, International University Publications, 1973) - and:

> Haas, Michael, ed.: International organization: an interdisciplinary bibliography. (Stanford, Hoover Institution Press, 1973).

For serials, reference may also be made to the "Index of publications of international organizations" in Ulrich's international periodicals directory and the similarly named index in the companion Irregular serials and annuals, an international directory (both works are published biennially, in alternate years, by Bowker of New York).

Since 1950 there has been a regularly issued (but variously titled) Catalog of publications issued by the Pan American Union and its successor the Organization of American States' General secretariat: this is currently an annual. A select list of recent OAS publications also appears at the back of each quarter's Inter-American review of bibliography.

Library catalogues

Printed library catalogues are themselves standard bibliographical sources - especially those of the British Library Reference Division (the former British Museum Library) and the United States National Union Catalog. See the section 'PRINTED CATALOGUES'.

Most libraries also include government publications in their subject catalogues. One of the most important of these, which has been published and kept up-to-date with regular (currently annual) supplements is the London bibliography of the social sciences (see: 'PRINTED CATALOGUES').

Official publications

Library catalogues (cont'd.)

For a discussion of the inconsistencies of library practice
in arranging government publications in catalogues, see:

> Hixon, Jean: "Latin American serial documents:
> what form of entry, what is 'official'?", Eighth
> Seminar on the Acquisition of Latin American
> Library Materials, Madison (Wis.), 1963 (work-
> ing paper 4, pp.101-112 of vol 2 of the Final
> report).

Special types of official publications discussed elsewhere

There are separate sections on 'CENSUSES', 'LAW &
LEGISLATION' and 'STATISTICS'. For archival material,
see: 'MANUSCRIPTS & ARCHIVES'.

Specialising libraries

Libraries with large general collections of Latin American
official publications include those of the London School of
Economics, Cambridge University, the Foreign and Commonwealth Office and the Official Publications Library of the
British Library Reference Division. The last named has the
largest collection, particularly of pre-1900 and post-1940
material; most of its holdings of 1920-1946 publications lie
uncatalogued in the Woolwich depository but may be obtained for readers upon request. Many other libraries are
strong in official publications on their respective fields of
interest (consult Bernard Naylor's Directory of libraries
and special collections on Latin America and the West
Indies, Athlone Press, 1975).

The publications of the U.N. and its agencies are systematically collected by the British Library, the National Library of Wales, the U.N. Information Centre and by the libraries of the London School of Economics, the Royal Institute of International Affairs, and the Institute of Development Studies at the University of Sussex.

Specialising libraries (cont'd.)

O.A.S. publications are systematically acquired by the
libraries of the London School of Economics, the Royal
Institute of International Affairs and the University of
Leicester.

[JG]

PATENTS & TRADEMARKS

Patents as a source of information

It is an essential preliminary to the tackling of a new problem to find out what other workers have already done in the same field. This information can be used to discover ways in which a problem has been tackled in the past, and also to check whether a possible solution has already been developed and patented. Patent specifications often disclose technical information much earlier than in other literature.

Once a patent has lapsed the invention set out in the complete specification may be fully utilized, provided there is no infringement of other existing patents.

A complete specification is a document that contains (a) a full and sufficient disclosure to enable any person, skilled in the art concerned, to understand and carry out the invention and (b) a clear statement of the monopoly sought.

Patent procedure varies widely from country to country, as does the method of publication, and the period for which the patent is valid. See:

> Baxter, John Walker: World patent law and practice, 2.ed. (London, Sweet and Maxwell, 1973) - and:

> Manual for the handling of applications for patents, designs and trade marks throughout the world. (Amsterdam, Octrooibureau los en Stigter) - looseleaf, updated by supplements.

There is also a short account of the international aspects of patents and trade marks on pages 456-468 of the article "Patent and trademark office, U.S." in volume 21 of the Encyclopedia of library and information science, edited by Allen Kent and others, (New York & Basle, Dekker, 1977).

Patents & trademarks

Availability of patents

Brazil is the only Latin American country whose Patent Office publishes complete specifications. The others issue abridgements only, usually in their official gazette (see the paragraph on these under 'LAW & LEGISLATION').

British patents, abridgements and related publications may be consulted, free, at the Holborn branch of the Science Reference Library (SRL) at 25 Southampton Buildings, Chancery Lane, London WC2. Foreign patents and official journals are available across the road in the SRL's Chancery House Annexe: They are mostly on open access, except for some closed sets and older publications, which can be supplied on request.

Some British and foreign patents can also be consulted at other libraries in the U.K., although no significant collections of Latin American specifications exist outside the SRL. See:

> Great Britain. Department of trade: Patents - a source of technical information, prepared by the Department of Trade and the Central Office of Information. (London, HMSO, 1975).

Elsewhere in Europe, West Germany, with its close commercial links with Latin America, seems to have the best collections, particularly from the more industrially developed countries, Brazil, Mexico and Venezuela. See:

> Commission of the European Communities: Patent information and documentation. (Munich, Verlag Dokumentation, 1960).

Present state of SRL holdings

Most foreign patents and official journals held at SRL are obtained through exchange agreements with foreign governments and government departments. Whatever the source, however, it is often difficult to ensure regularity and

Patents & trademarks

Present state of SRL holdings (cont'd.)

continuity of supply, and many sets will be found to be incomplete. The reasons have been discussed at many of the
annual Seminars on the Acquisition of Latin American Library Materials (SALALM's), and also in:

> Landau, Maria J.: "Acquisition of Latin Ameri-
> can scientific literature in the Science Refer-
> ence Library", Libri, 25(4), Oct. 1975, pp.318-
> 323 - and in:

> Ligue des Bibliothèques Européennes de Re-
> cherche: Acquisitions from the Third World:
> papers of the LIBER seminar 17-19 September
> 1973, edited by Derek A. Clarke. (London,
> Mansell, 1975).

The SRL is the only U.K. library with significant holdings
of Latin American patents, and the only one apart from the
Official Publications Library (the old State Paper Room of
the British Museum) with significant holdings of Latin
American official gazettes.

SRL holdings - Brazil

In marked contrast to its neighbours, Brazil is of world importance in patent and trademark publishing. It is one of
only ten countries (including the U.K., the U.S.A. and
Canada) whose patents are regularly covered in Chemical
abstracts. Brazilian patents are also included in Derwent
publications Inc.'s World patents index.

The SRL's holdings of Brazilian patent and trademark information go back (under a variety of titles) to 1893. Full
patent specifications have been received since their publication began in 1971, but holdings are not complete.

The Revista da propriedade industrial (held since the first
issue in 1972) is section 3 of the Diario oficial and is divided into two parts: patents and trademarks. Both parts are

SRL holdings - Brazil (cont'd.)

informative, the patents section containing published applications in numerical and class order, with date of applica-
tion, title of invention, name of patentee, inventor and firm;
applications granted are also listed.

Other publications of the Departamento Nacional da Propriedade Industrial held at SRL include Patentes brasileiras
extintas (1966-   ) and Patentes de invenção do DNPI
(1969-   ) which is part 3 of the DNPI's Documentação e
informação. For details see:

> Kase, Francis J.: Foreign patents, a guide to
> official patent literature. (Dobbs Ferry NY,
> Oceana, 1972).

SRL holdings - major Spanish American countries

Argentina, despite a declining output of scientific literature,
has maintained a steady output of patent information. The
Publicación oficial of Argentina's Dirección Nacional de la
Propiedad Industrial has been received at SRL since 1955,
and there are issues under earlier titles and in different
formats that go back as far as 1868.

The Colombian Gaceta de la propiedad industrial is an irregular publication, currently received at SRL, which began in
1958. The SRL also has earlier issues from 1930 under
other titles. The Gaceta has sections on patents (only brief
extracts without summaries or drawings), on trademarks
and on industrial designs. Between 1924 and 1928 Colombian
patents and trademarks appeared in the Diario oficial.

Mexico's monthly Gaceta de la propiedad industrial has been
received at SRL since it began in 1930, but is now arriving
four years in arrears. It is divided into patents, trademarks,
slogans and trade names; each part is fully informative - including, for instance, abstracts of granted patents with full
filing details. For the period before 1930, SRL has the same
information in a variety of publications that go back to 1891.

Patents & trademarks

SRL holdings - major Spanish American countries (cont'd.)

For Peru, SRL holds El Peruano: diario oficial from 1919 to 1969 (and the earlier Registro oficial de fomento) providing both patent and trademark information. Later issues are in the Official Publications Library, which is now, like the SRL, part of the Reference Division of the British Library.

Venezuela, a founder-member of OPEC (the Organization of Petroleum Exporting Countries) might be expected to be among the better documented states, for patent output usually reflects a nation's commercial and industrial development. In fact the SRL has been able to obtain little up-to-date information. The Boletín de la propiedad industrial (formerly ... de la propiedad industrial y comercial), which began in 1931 and gives information on both patents (short extracts only) and trademarks, has not arrived since 1968.

SRL holdings - other Spanish American countries

The Gaceta oficial de Bolivia contains patent abridgements and trademarks. SRL holdings are up-to-date and go back to 1937 (prior to 1964 under different titles).

The Costa Rican Diario oficial covering patents and trademarks is held from 1936 to 1972.

The Cuban Boletín oficial is held from 1906. Contents have varied but current issues (1977 has been received) contain sections on patents and trademarks.

Holdings from the Dominican Republic, Ecuador and Guatemala are sparse, and nothing has been received for the last 25 years.

Patents & trademarks

SRL holdings - other Spanish American countries (cont'd.)

Uruguay's Diario oficial, containing patents and trademarks, has been received regularly at SRL since 1936, and prior to that, other publications covering the same subjects are also held.

[MJL - with acknowledgements to Miss Helena Chicken, Research Assistant, Foreign Patents Section, SRL, for help in the search for relevant material]

PERIODICALS

Definition

Any publication intended to appear in an indefinitely continued number of parts is, in library jargon, a serial. Any
serial that aspires (however ineffectually) to some degree
of regularity is a periodical, a catch-all term embracing
anything from an annual reference work to a daily newspaper. Newspapers (with which we have conveniently grouped a variety of other news sources) are discussed elsewhere, under 'NEWS & CURRENT AFFAIRS'. Annual
reference works are relegated to our 'HANDBOOKS &
GUIDES' section, except for the special category 'DIREC-
TORIES'. National bibliographies (mostly annual in publication) are also treated elsewhere, as are all officially published periodicals - see: 'NATIONAL BIBLIOGRAPHY' and
'OFFICIAL PUBLICATIONS', respectively. All other periodicals, from popular magazines to learned journals, are
dealt with below.

The residue of irregular serials you may find treated by
libraries sometimes as books, sometimes as periodicals.

Citation

Although periodicals are usually cited by name, library
cataloguers often prefer to list them under their publisher
or sponsoring body if this forms part of the name, e.g.:
'Society for Latin American Studies: Bulletin'. This arrangement is subject to the further complication that many libraries list all institutions under the "place" (usually the
city) where located; e.g. 'Rio de Janeiro. Biblioteca nacional: Anuário'.

The British Museum General catalogue has 'Periodical
publications' as a special heading and, with the exception of
those issued by governments, institutions and societies,
arranges them all by place under this general head, although
there are cross-references from the actual titles).

Periodicals

Citation (cont'd.)

Some catalogues choose to ignore prepositions and articles within a title, and some even ignore minor spelling differences, so you might (for instance) find 'Boletim do', 'Boletim para', 'Boletín de', 'Boletín del', 'Boletín para', 'Bulletin for', 'Bulletin of the' and 'Bulletin pour la' all filed together as 'Bulletin'.

When a periodical changes it name (a quite frequent occurrence) you may find all references to it under its latest title, or under its earliest title, or the two (or more) titles may be treated as separate publications. Entry under the latest title is probably commonest.

Systems of periodical numbering also vary. Some periodicals give each volume its own sequence of part numbers; others continue the part numbering independently of the volume numbers. (In a like manner, pages may be numbered separately for each part, or consecutively for the entire volume). Latin American journals often have a sequence of year ('anno', 'ano', 'año') numbering over and above the volume numbering, and occasionally the volumes are divided (or grouped) into tomes ('tomos'). When a periodical changes its coverage, its policy, its frequency , etc., or revives after a period of dormancy, or undergoes some other major or minor metamorphosis, this may be marked by starting a new series ('era', 'época', 'círculo' etc.), which may or may not be accompanied by a new sequence of year/volume/tome/ part numbers.

The financial and other difficulties which beset periodicals, particularly Latin American ones, cause many irregularities that may be reflected in their numbering. Often double- or even triple-numbered parts are issued to make up for publication gaps. Periodicals in difficulties have even been known to lose count of themselves and issue two parts with the same number, or omit a number altogether. Ruses to evade censorship difficulties may also produce their own complications. There is also a custom to issue the first

Citation (cont'd.)

number as a kite flier and call it 'volume one, number zero'.

We can only urge you to check carefully any references, beware of over-trusting bibliographies and catalogues, and make your own references as explicit as possible by specifying year, volume and part numbers, and by giving the date of issue as well.

Identification: bibliographies

A good starting point, especially if you are looking for somewhere to get an article published, is:

> Birkos, Alexander S., and Tambs, L.A.: Academic writer's guide to periodicals. Volume 1: Latin American studies. (Kent, Ohio, Kent State University Press, 1971).

This is limited to periodicals accepting articles in English. For periodicals originating in Latin America itself, the best annotated listing is probably:

> Zimmerman, Irene: A guide to current Latin American periodicals: humanities and social sciences. (Gainesville, Fla., Kallman, 1961).

A more comprehensive list, but one that is now alas almost twenty years out-of-date is:

> Pan American Union: Repertorio de publicaciones periódicas actuales latinoamericanos / Directory of current Latin American periodicals ... (Paris, UNESCO, 1958).

Periodicals

Identification: bibliographies (cont'd.)

Specialised, but more recent are:

América latina: liste mondiale des périodiques spécialisés. (Paris, Maison des sciences de l'homme/Mouton, 1974);

Bleznick, Donald W.: "A guide to journals in the Hispanic field: a selected annotated list of journals central to the study of Spanish and Spanish-American language and literature", Hispania, 52 (Nov. 1969), pp.723-737;

Pan American Union, Department of scientific affairs, and, Centro de documentación científica y técnica de México: Guide to Latin American scientific and technical periodicals, an annotated list. (Washington, the Union, 1962) - also issued in Spanish;

Sable, Martin H.: Periodicals for Latin American development, trade and finance: an annotated bibliography. (Los Angeles, Latin American Center of UCLA, 1965);

Sociedad argentina de bibliotecarios de instituciones sociales, científicas, artísticas y técnicas: Catálogo colectivo de publicaciones periódicas existentes en bibliotecas científicas y técnicas argentinas, 2.ed., dirigida por Ernesto Gustavo Gietz. (Buenos Aires, Consejo nacional de investigaciones científicas y técnicas, 1962?, plus later supplements).

There are useful, but unannotated lists of 'revistas científicas' and of 'periódicos y boletines' on pages 33-36 of:

Mörner, Magnus, and Campa, R.: Investigación en ciencias sociales e históricas sobre América latina: enfoque preliminar para una guía. (Rome, CEISAL, 1975).

Periodicals

Identification: bibliographies (cont'd.)

For Latin American academic journals there is:

> Levi, Nadi: Guía de publicaciones periódicas de
> universidades latinoamericanas. (Mexico City,
> UNAM, 1967).

There are also various guides to the periodical output of
individual countries. For example, Spanish periodicals on
Latin America are listed in:

> Beckman, Jan D.: Dokumentation der spanischen
> Lateinamerika-Forschung. (Hamburg, FRG,
> 1971).

See also the titles in the paragraph 'Location' below.

Keeping up-to-date

News of new periodical titles appears in the SALALM Newsletter (Austin, Texas, the SALALM Secretariat), and in
many booksellers' catalogues.

A more difficult problem is that of determining whether a
particular title is still being published. Few periodicals ever
announce an imminent demise; indeed, in most cases the
publisher will always be in hope of finding means to continue,
and many a title has suddenly revived after months, or even
years, of non-appearance. In the fields of science and technology you can learn of new periodicals and of changes to
existing ones (cessation, amalgamation, title change etc.)
from the four-weekly Periodicals news of the British Library's Science Reference Library. Otherwise, the best one
can do is to check annual or other frequently revised lists of
current periodicals. International lists such as Ulrich's
international periodicals directory and its associated Irregular serials and annuals (the two published in alternate
years by Bowker of New York) are useful for the more
widely known titles, but for anything obscure it is better to

Periodicals

Identification: bibliographies (cont'd.)

consult a Latin American source. A Uruguayan publisher
has recently begun an annual mimeographed list of Latin
American titles:

> Revistero: international periodicals directory
> C.B.A. (Montevideo, Darino, 1975-   ).

There are also sources for individual countries, and many
libraries issue printed or mimeographed lists of titles they
currently receive; there is, for instance, the "Annual list of
serials" issued as a supplement to the Library of Congress
Accessions List, Brazil, which records all serials currently
being acquired by the Library of Congress Office in Rio de
Janeiro.

Location

For various reasons, libraries tend to be less conscientious
in notifying the BRITISH UNION CATALOGUE OF LATIN
AMERICANA (q.v.) of their periodical acquisitions than of
their new books. BUCLA has nevertheless issued, as a
special supplement to its New Latin American titles:

> University of London. Institute of Latin American
> studies: Latin American periodicals, a union list
> of the holdings of six British universities. (Lon-
> don, the Institute, 1970) - the six are Cambridge,
> Essex, Glasgow, Liverpool, London and Oxford.

Giving rather more bibliographical details, and covering the
periodical holdings of many more libraries, is the series of
Latin American serials compiled by the Committee on Latin
America (COLA). Three have been published; more are
planned (the next to be on science and technology):

> Committee on Latin America: Latin American
> Economic and social serials, edited by K.I. Porter.
> (London, Bingley, 1969);

Periodicals

Location (cont'd.)

Committee on Latin America: Latin American
history with politics - a serials list, edited by
C[hristopher] J. Koster. (Farnborough, Hants.,
Gregg International, 1973, distributed by Latin
America Books of York);

Committee on Latin America: Latin American
serials, 3: Literature with language, art and
music, edited by L[aurence] Hallewell. (London, COLA, 1977).

The published catalogues of individual libraries sometimes
include periodicals (see 'PRINTED CATALOGUES'). An
important recent one is that of the Latin American Center of
Stanford (California) University, which records 110 journals
received at Stanford between March 1969 and March 1970:

Latin America: a guide to periodical literature.
(New York, Center for Inter-American Relations,
1972).

There is also the general British union catalogue of periodicals (BUCOP) - see the section 'INTER-LIBRARY LEN-
DING' - and its American equivalent, the Union list of
serials and supplements, entitled New serial titles.

Indexes

Each of the COLA volumes just mentioned includes an article by A. J. Walford and others on periodical indexes. Each
article covers general indexes and then discusses those
especially relevant to the special subjects of the volume.

Since these were written, the "International bibliography of
cumulative indexes to journals publishing articles on Hispanic languages and literatures" by Zubatsky, mentioned in
volume 3, has been continued and expanded by:

Periodicals

Indexes (cont'd.)

> Zubatsky, David S.: "A bibliography of cumulative indexes to Latin American humanities and social science journals of the nineteenth and twentieth centuries", SALALM Newsletter, 3(4)-4(2), June-December 1976.

The SALALM Newsletter 4(1), September 1976 (pp.12-18) contains information on the important Hispanic American periodical index (HAPI), including a full list of the periodicals it is currently indexing.

Also omitted from the COLA articles is the section on West Indian literature articles (pp.270-281) in:

> New, William H.: Critical writings on Commonwealth literatures: a selective bibliography to 1970 ... (University Park, Pennsylvania State University Press, 1975).

To be published in December 1977 is the subject catalogue of the Ibero-American Institute in West Berlin which includes entries for periodical articles in the humanities and natural sciences (particularly medicine) from over 2,000 journals:

> Ibero-Amerikanisches Institut, Berlin: Schlagwortkatalog des Ibero-Amerikanischen Instituts preussischer Kulturbesitz in Berlin. (Boston, Mass., Hall, 30 vols, 1977).

Periodicals of the English-speaking Caribbean are now being indexed in the quarterly Carindex (St. Augustine, Trinidad, University of the West Indies Trinidad campus, 1977-   ).

For further data on periodical indexes, see the section "Indexes" in:

Indexes (cont'd.)

Gropp, Arthur E.: A bibliography of Latin American bibliographies. (Metuchen, Scarecrow, 1968, and supplement, 1971) - which has been supplemented in turn by:

Cordeiro, Daniel R.: "A bibliography of Latin American bibliographies", Twenty-first Seminar on the acquisition of Latin American library materials, Bloomington (Ind.), 1976 (Working paper A-2).

Offprints

Rember that a periodical article is often also issued separately, usually as an 'offprint'; check for this in the Author catalogue. Libraries may also keep photo-copies of periodical articles: enquire whether these are included in the main catalogue.

[LH]

PRINTED CATALOGUES

The National Union Catalog (N.U.C.)

What began as the printed catalogue of the Library of [the U.S.] Congress has now been expanded into a union catalogue of all major American and Canadian libraries, and can be expected to contain almost every publication on or from Latin America issued in recent years (i.e. since the mid-sixties) and a very significant proportion of those of earlier years.

The basic work is an author listing of "Pre-1956" imprints, in several hundred folio volumes; publication began in 1968 and is now within sight of completion. (The unpublished part is largely covered by the earlier series of Library of Congress published catalogues).

Works published after 1955 are listed in a series of supplements: 1956-1967 in 125 volumes, 1968-1972 in 119. Thereafter the programme is one of monthly parts, cumulated quarterly, annually and five-yearly. It is important to remember that dates after 1956 are those of cataloguing, not of publication: Latin American books will usually be found in the section covering a period some 18 to 36 months after their imprint date.

Not only is the N.U.C. unsurpassed as an author bibliography; it is also issued in the form of a subject catalogue. Unfortunately, for obvious reasons of cost, this will seldom be found in British libraries.

The Library of Congress also provides a service of cataloguing data on cards in advance of publication in the N.U.C. One of the few U.K. subscribers is the London Institute of Latin American Studies (see: 'BRITISH UNION CATALOGUE OF LATIN AMERICANA'). The catalogue is also available in machine-readable format; see: 'DATA BANKS & INFORMATION IN MACHINE READABLE FORMAT'.

Printed catalogues

The British Museum Catalogue

Although the General catalogue of printed books of what
used to be the British Museum Library (now the British
Library Reference Division) has now been almost dwarfed
by the National Union Catalog, it remains the second biggest bibliographic tool in our libraries, and the Latin Americanist will find it particularly useful for the period of the
Museum's affluence (viz. pre-World War I, and particularly,
pre-1880). Its holdings of mid-19th century material from
the region are still unsurpassed by any North American collection. Like the NUC, its basic 263 volumes cover the
"Pre-1956" period. Supplements cover 1956-1965, and five-
yearly periods thereafter: as with the NUC the later dates
are those of cataloguing, not of publication.

The British Museum cataloguing style was established early
last century, which produces certain idiosyncrasies. Its
category headings, for instance, require you to search for
almanacs under 'Ephemerides', and for periodicals under
'Periodical publications', a heading which is sub-arranged
by place of publication.

There is also a Subject index of modern books acquired by
the British Museum Library, in five-yearly parts, covering
from 1881.

The Newspaper library now has its own Catalogue of the
Newspaper Library, Colindale, issued in 1975.

British National Bibliography (BNB)

A copy of every new British or Irish publication has to be
sent to the Copyright Receipt Office of the British Library.
Apart from music, maps, Irish government publications and
certain U.K. government publications of a routine nature,
all of them are then listed in the Bibliographic Services Division's weekly British National Bibliography.

Printed catalogues

British National Bibliography (BNB) (cont'd.)

The BNB is arranged by subject, according to the Dewey
Decimal Classification (the scheme used in most public libraries). There is an author index each week, and the last
issue of each month has a subject index and a cumulated
author index. The entire work (classified list and author and
subject indexes) is cumulated four-monthly, annually and
three-yearly.

Since most important North American works nowadays have
simultaneous publication in this country, the BNB provides a
unique source of information on English language publications, on Latin America (as on any other subject). Remember when using the subject index to look not only under 'Latin
America' but also under 'Caribbean region', 'Central America', 'South America', 'West Indies' and the names of individual countries.

The BNB began in January 1950 as an independent organisation: this is why its cataloguing practice is completely different from that of the (former) British Museum Library. It
does however function as a current supplement to the
B.M.G.K. in respect of English-language material, and the
cataloguing practice of the B.N.B. is in fact increasingly
becoming the norm for the whole British Library organisation.

G.K. Hall Catalogues

Almost all the major collections of Latin Americana in North
American and European libraries have had their catalogues
reproduced in book form by G.K. Hall & Co. of Boston, Mass.
Most of them are in dictionary-catalogue form (i.e. author,
subject and sometimes title entries in one combined sequence), thus providing excellent subject as well as author
bibliographies. They are also up-dated by regular supplements - those of the important Latin American Collection of
the University of Texas appear every other year.

Printed catalogues

G. K. Hall Catalogues (cont'd.)

Details of Hall's American library catalogues will be found on pages 18-21 of:

> Haro, Robert P.: Latin American research in the United States and Canada. (Chicago, American Library Association, 1971).

Too recent for inclusion in Haro are:

> Joint library of the International Monetary Fund and the International Bank for Reconstruction and Development, Washington: The developing areas, a classed bibliography of the Joint Bank-Fund Library. Volume 1: Latin America and the Caribbean. (Boston, Hall, 1976) - and:

> University of Miami, Coral Gables: Catalog of the Cuban and Caribbean Library. (Boston, Hall, 1977).

The only British library to have had its catalogue issued in Hall's Latin American series is the Canning House Library of the Hispanic and Luso-Brazilian Council. This appeared in 1967 in two parts: Hispanic and Luso-Brazilian, as at that time there were separate Hispanic and Luso-Brazilian Councils. Each part is divided into author and subject sections, and each has had (to date) a single supplement.

Hall have also issued the catalogue of Europe's largest Latin American collection:

> Ibero-Amerikanisches Institut, Berlin: Schlagwort-katalog des Ibero-Amerikanischen Instituts preussischer Kulturbesitz in Berlin. (Boston, Mass., Hall, 30 vols, 1977) - a subject, geographical and biographical index, in English and Spanish, to 300,000 volumes, mostly post-1945, and to periodical articles from some 2,000 journals, making a grand total of 470,000 cards, photographically reproduced in book form.

Printed catalogues

Other library catalogues

One of the few North American catalogues in the field not
produced by Hall is the Widener Library shelflist of Harvard University Library of which numbers 5 & 6, "Latin
America, and Latin American periodicals" in two volumes,
were issued in 1966, and number 21, "Latin American literature" appeared in 1969. Both consist of brief author and title
entries arranged according to the library's own classification
scheme, with author and subject indexes, a chronological
listing and a schedule of the subject classification. The publisher, naturally, was Harvard University Press.

Also very useful for its coverage of the region is A London
bibliography of the social sciences, the subject catalogue of
the British Library of Political and Economic Science and the
Edward Fry Library of International Law (both at the London
School of Economics). The basic work in 4 volumes covers
holdings up to 1929, and includes the stocks of several other
libraries. The eight supplements to 1973 cover varying
periods; since then there have been annual supplements.
There is an author index down to 1936 only.

Recent accessions lists: U.K. libraries

A select list of recent acquisitions by U.K. libraries has
been published since 1968 by the Institute of Latin American
Studies, London, as New Latin American titles, but this is
shortly to be replaced by a series of subject bibliographies.

West Indian material appears in the London Institute of Commonwealth Studies' quarterly Accessions list (1949? -   )
and in the Quarterly list of accessions (1950-   ) of its
Oxford University namesake.

Recent accessions lists: European libraries

The Ibero-Amerikanisches Institut in Berlin issues a regular
Neuerwerbungen der Bibliothek arranged by broad subject
groupings.

Printed catalogues

Recent accessions lists: European libraries   (cont'd.)

The Amsterdam Centrum voor studie en dokumentatie van
Latijns Amerika ('CEDLA') issues a union Catalogus on
microfiche, listing material added to Dutch academic libraries by author, country and subject, with an English index.

The Paris Institut des hautes études de l'Amérique latine's
library publishes a six-monthly Acquisitions récentes, arranged by country and sub-arranged by broad subject headings.

Recent accessions lists: North American libraries

A regular Accessions list is issued by the library of the
Land Tenure Center of the University of Wisconsin, Madison,
and Michigan State University issues Latin America: select
recent accessions.

Recent accessions lists: Latin America

Brazilian imprints acquired for the Library of Congress by
its Rio de Janeiro Office are listed in its bi-monthly Library
of Congress accessions list Brazil.

Another important library accessions list is that of the
United Nations Economic Commission for Latin America
('ECLA' or 'CEPAL') in Santiago de Chile.

[LH]

SOCIETIES & ASSOCIATIONS

Importance

To quote the introduction to the Encyclopedia of associations (Detroit, Gale, 1975): "associations and professional societies ... are unsurpassed as 'switch-boards' connecting persons needing information to highly qualified sources of information. Frequently, a 'phone call or letter ... produces more information - faster - than any amount of research in printed books and periodicals". Unfortunately such organisations are apt to operate with volunteer staff and small budgets (so SAE's with all enquiries). They are also likely to change secretaries and addresses quite often. Current addresses should therefore be checked, either in the latest edition of the Encyclopedia of associations (mainly, but not solely, concerned with North America) or the annual Directory of British associations and associations in Ireland (Beckenham, Kent, CBD Research), or, whenever possible, in the current issue of the society's journal or bulletin.

The following list of societies directly concerned with Latin America aims to be complete for the U.K., but is very selective for the rest of the world.

In the United Kingdom

Anglo-Argentine Society: 2, Belgrave Square, London SW1X 8PJ;

Anglo-Brazilian Society: 2, Belgrave Square, London SW1X 8PJ;

Anglo-Chilean Society: 12, Devonshire Street, London W1N 2DS;

Anglo-Colombian Society: 5, Belgrave Square, London SW1;

Anglo-Peruvian Society: 52, Sloane Street, London SW1X 9SP;

Societies & associations

Association of teachers of Spanish and Portuguese
(publishes Vida hispánica): R.P.Clarke, Hon.
Sec., 33, North Lane, Huntington, Yorkshire;

Brazilian Chamber of Commerce in Great Britain:
35, Dover Street, London W1X   3RA;

British and Irish Development Studies Association:
c/o Institute of Development Studies, University
of Sussex, Falmer, Brighton, Sussex BN1 9RE;

British Mexican Society: 52, Grosvenor Gardens,
London SW1;

British Society for Caribbean Studies: Hon.Sec.:
Dr.Colin G.Clarke, Department of Geography, University of Liverpool;

British Uruguayan Society: Shreelane, 222 Brook-
lands Road, Weybridge, Surrey;

Committee on Latin America (COLA): G.H.Green,
BA, MBE, Hon.Sec., 2, Belgrave Square,
London SW1X 8PJ;

Falkland Islands Committee: 16 Regency Street,
London SW1;

Hispanic & Luso-Brazilian Council (publishes
British bulletin of publications on Latin America,
the West Indies, Spain and Portugal): 2, Belgrave
Square, London SW1X 8PJ;

Society for Latin American Studies (SLAS)
(publishes Bulletin ...): Paul Goulder, Hon.
Sec.: Department of Economics, City of
London Polytechnic, 84, Moorgate,
London EC2M 6SQ;

Societies & associations

In the United Kingdom (cont'd.)

Standing Conference of National and University Libraries. Latin American Group (SCONUL-LAG): Dr. L. Hallewell, Hon. Sec./Treasurer, the Library, School of Oriental and African Studies, Malet Street, London WC1E 7HP;

West India Committee: 18, Grosvenor Street, London W1X 0HP;

Working Party on Library Holdings of Commonwealth Literature: Michael Foster, Sec./Treasurer, Commonwealth Institute, Kensington High Street, London W8 6NQ.

Exiles' organisations in this country

Argentine Support Movement: 1, Cambridge Terrace, London NW1;

Chile Solidarity Campaign: 129, Seven Sisters Road, London N7;

Committee for Human Rights in Bolivia: 16, Ribblesdale Road, London N8 7EP;

Latin American Centre: 17, Hoxton Square, London N1;

Paraguay Committee: c/o 1, Cambridge Terrace, London NW1;

Uruguay Libre: 1, Cambridge Terrace, London NW1.

International pressure groups based in London

Mentioned because of their frequent involvement with developments in Latin America:

Amnesty International: 55, Theobalds Road, London WC1;

Societies & associations

International pressure groups based in London (cont'd.)

Survival International: 36, Craven Street, London
WC2 - concerned with the plight of aboriginal
races in Amazonia and elsewhere;

Writers and Scholars International (publishes
Index on censorship): 21, Russell Street,
London WC2B 5HP.

Societies in North America

Academy of American Franciscan History (publishes Americas): PO Box 34440, Washington
DC 20034, USA;

American Association of Teachers of Spanish and
Portuguese (publishes Hispania): Wichita State
University, Wichita KS 67208, USA;

Asociación Canadiense de Hispanistas (publishes:
Revista canadiense de estudios hispánicos);
Administration: Professor C. A. Marsden, De-
partment of Spanish, Carleton University,
Ottawa, Ont.K1S 5B6, Canada;

Canadian Association of Latin American Studies
(CALA) (publishes: Northsouth/Nordsud/
Nortesur/Nortesul): University of Toronto,
Toronto 181, Ont. M5S 1A1, Canada;

Conference of Latin American Geographers (CLAG):
Department of Geography, Saunders Hall, Uni-
versity of North Carolina, Chapel Hill NC 27514,
USA;

Conference on Latin American History (publishes:
Hispanic American historical review): Center
for Latin America, University of Wisconsin,
Milwaukee WI 53201, USA;

Societies & associations

Societies in North America   (cont'd.)

Hispanic Society of America: 15500 Broadway,
New York NY 10032, USA;

Inter-American Bibliographical and Library
Association (publishes: Doors to Latin
America): Box 583, North Miami Beach
FL 33160, USA;

Latin American Studies Association (LASA)
(publishes: Latin American research review
and Latin American studies newsletter):
Box 13362, University Station, Gainesville
FL 32604, USA;

Seminar on the Acquisition of Latin American
Library Materials (SALALM) (publishes:
SALALM Newsletter): SALALM Secretariat,
Benson Library, University of Texas at
Austin, Austin TX 78712, USA.

Societies of continental Europe

Arbeitsgemeinschaft Deutsche Lateinamerika-
Forschung (ADLAF) (publishes: Informationsdienst): Hamburg, German Federal Republic;

Consejo Europeo de Investigaciones Sociales sobre
América Latina (CEISAL): Dr. Harold Blake-
more coordinador general, Institute of Latin
American Studies, 31 Tavistock Square,
London WC1H 9HA;

Schweizerische Amerikanisten-Gesellschaft/
Société Suisse des Américanistes (publishes
Bulletin): Musée d'Ethnographie, 65-67,
Boulevard Carl-Vogt, 1205 Geneva.

Societies & associations

British trade associations in Latin America

Asociación venezolano-británica de comercio e
industria: Edificio Blandin, Piso 1, Oficina 1c,
Apartado 5713, Caracas;

British Chamber of Commerce in Brazil: Caixa
postal 1621, 01000 São Paulo SP;

British Chamber of Commerce in the Argentine
Republic, Inc.: Veinticinco de Mayo 444,
Piso 5, Buenos Aires;

British-Chilean Chamber of Commerce: Calle
Bandera 84, Oficina 408, Casilla 536, Santiago;

Cámara de Comercio Británica AC: Rio Tiber 106,
Piso 6, Mexico 5, DF;

Cámara de Comercio Uruguayo-británica: Avenida
Agraciada 1641, Piso 2, Escitorio 201F,
Montevideo.

Societies in Latin America and the West Indies

Association of Caribbean university, research
and institutional libraries (ACURIL) (publishes: Carta informativa): Secretary for
1978: Rosa Q. Mesa, University Library,
University of Florida, Gainesville FL 32601,
USA;

Caribbean archives association: c/o Archives de
Guadeloupe, Basse-Terre, Guadeloupe,
French West Indies.

For other societies, consult the sources suggested in our
section on 'DIRECTORIES'.

Societies & associations

Institutions

For addresses of institutions (i.e. organizations with fixed locations and permanent headquarters), see the paragraph 'Research institutes' in our section on 'UNIVERSITY STUDY & RESEARCH', and the section 'DIRECTORIES'.

Conferences

See the section 'CONFERENCES & MEETINGS'.

Latin America Bureau

As we go to press our attention is drawn to a new organisation, the Latin America Bureau, of PO Box 134, London NW1 4JY, and concerned with 'research and action on Latin America in the fields of human rights and related social, political and economic issues'.

[LH]

STATISTICS

How published

Central governments have always been the principal
gatherers and diffusers of statistical information, but not all
official data is necessarily collected or presented by a country's national statistical office. Although certain fields (customs returns, for example) are often the latter's exclusive
responsibility, many other government agencies, at national,
provincial and even municipal levels, may well have their
own statistical units to deal with sectoral or local data.
Central banks and branches of private industry may also
compile and publish statistics in their own fields.

Those who require maximum detail should be aware that
much data is no longer made available in conventional form;
see: 'DATA BANKS ...'

General sources

Practically every Latin American country issues a summary
Anuario estadístico - Portuguese: estatístico - which is adequate for many purposes. As we go to press we learn that
Inter Documentation Company of Zug, Switzerland plans to
make these available for all mainland South American countries except Bolivia, Chile, Panama and Surinam, on microfiche, together with annual reports of the national bank and
the national budget.

Even more general are the various international statistical
publications, most of which are merely summary compilations of national statistics (although some regional integra-
tion and trade organisations, such as ALALC and CARIFTA
do have their own exclusive sources).

The principal general compilations for Latin America are:

> América en cifras, 1960-   (Washington,
> General secretariat of OAS, biennial);

Statistics

General sources (cont'd.)

Anuario estadístico de America latina/
Statistical yearbook for Latin America,
1973-   (Santiago de Chile, Comisión
económica para América latina, annual?);

Statistical abstract of Latin America, 1955-
(Los Angeles, UCLA Center of Latin American
Studies, annual, but none published 1958-59).

Guides to statistical organisation

Although there are few descriptive, let alone methodologically critical, accounts of the statistical systems of the region, there do exist comparatively recent works for five important countries:

Gleason Galicia, Rubén: Las estadísticas y
censos de México, su organización y estado
actual.   (México, Instituto de investigaciones sociales de la UNAM, 1968);

Instituto Torcuato di Tella. Centro de investigaciones económicas: Catálogo de estadísticas
publicadas en la República argentina, 2.ed.
(Buenos Aires, 4 vols, 1966-68);

Mesa Lago, Carmelo: "Availability and reliability of statistics in socialist Cuba", Latin
American research review, 4(1), 1969, pp.53-
91 and 4(2), 1969, pp.47-81.

Towards full employment: a programme for
Colombia prepared by an inter-agency team
organised by the International Labour Office.
(Geneva, ILO, 1970) - Appendix 12: statistics,
pp.437-471;

Statistics

Guides to statistical organisation (cont'd.)

> Venegas Borges, Pedro Luis: El sistema
> estadística nacional, una institución en
> crisis. (Caracas, the author, 1974).

A useful general work is:

> Wilkie, James W.: Statistics and national
> policy. (Los Angeles, Latin American
> Center of UCLA, 1974).

Lists of organisations

From time to time national statistical offices and other
agencies issue catalogues or sales lists. These can be used
in conjunction with whatever explanatory material is included in the statistical publications themselves. It is most
important to watch for information on changes in procedures of data collection, analysis and presentation. Where
accessible published sources are inadequate, there is
probably no alternative to direct correspondence with the
issuing agency. In this respect, two guides are useful:

> Great Britain. Statistics and market intelli-
> gence library: National statistical offices of
> overseas countries. (London, the Library,
> 1973);
>
> Asociación latinoamericana de instituciones
> financieras de desarrollo: Directorio latino-
> americano de instituciones financieras. (Lima,
> the Association, 1972) - a members' list which
> excludes some central banks and only partly
> covers the Caribbean.

Statistics

Bibliographies

The Inter-American Statistical Institute has been responsible for:

> Statistical activities of the American nations 1940: a compendium of the statistical services and activities in twenty two nations ..., edited under the direction of the Temporary organizing committee of the I.A.S.I. by Elizabeth Phelps. (Washington, the Institute, 1941);

- and this is continued by a revised series of single country volumes:

> Inter American Statisticsl Institute: Actividades estadísticas de las naciones americanas, 1- (Washington, the Institute, 195-? -   );

the Institute has also issued:

> Inter American Statistical Institute: Bibliography of selected statistical sources of the American nations ..., a guide to the principal statistical materials of the twenty two American nations including data, analyses, methodology and law and organization of statistical agencies. (Washington, the Institute, 1947, reprinted Detroit, Ethridge, 1974) - arranged by country, subarranged by subject, with agency, title and subject indexes.

More up-to-date are:

> Johnson, Charles W.: Índice de cuadros estadísticos socio-políticos sobre America latina, 1946-1969. (Mexico City, Instituto de investigaciones sociales, 1972);

Bibliographies   (cont'd.)

> Joint Library of the International Monetary Fund
> and the International Bank for Reconstruction
> and Development, Washington: The developing
> areas, a classed bibliography of the Joint Bank-
> Fund Library. Volume 1: Latin America and the
> Caribbean.   (Boston, Mass., Hall, 1976).

> Montenegro, Tulio Hostilio: "Bibliografía ano-
> tada de las principales fuentes de estadísticas
> sobre América latina", Handbook of Latin
> American studies, 29 (1967), pp.613-639;

> Wilhelms, Christian, and Sedas, J.G.de A.:
> Quellenverzeichnis zur Wirtschaftsstatistik
> Iberoamerikas ...   (Hamburg, Institut für
> Iberoamerikakunde, 1966).

There is a "Bibliography of major general statistical publications of Latin America" included as an addendum to:

> Ford, Charlotte: "The reproduction of official
> Latin American census and statistical publica-
> tions for purchase by interested libraries:
> measures taken by the University of Florida
> Library", Tenth Seminar on the Acquisition of
> Latin American Library Materials, Detroit,
> 1965, (working paper 6).

Reference should also be made to works covering the wider
field of government publications in general - see the section
on 'OFFICIAL PUBLICATIONS'.

Serial bibliographies

Limited to bulletins, yearbooks and other serial publications are:

Statistics

Serial bibliographies (cont'd.)

> Sharma, Y.K. ed.: List of statistical yearbooks
> and bulletins published by governments, and
> annual reports and bulletins published by central
> banks, in the collections of selected U.S. librar-
> ies. (New Haven, Economic Growth Centre of
> Yale University, 1972);

> United Nations Library, Geneva: Catalogue of
> periodicals, annuals and special series cur-
> rently received at the U.N. library. (Geneva,
> Processing section of the library, 1972) - Part
> II is country list of government reports, statis-
> tical publications and official and unofficial
> annuals;

> United States of America. Library of Congress.
> Census library project: Statistical yearbooks, an
> annotated bibliography ..., prepared by Phyllis
> G. Carter. (Washington, GPO, 1953).

Phyllis Carter also contributed the section 'Statistics' to
each year's Handbook of Latin American Studies between
1948 and 1955 (volumes 14-21); since then notes on statistical publications have been scattered throughout each annual
volume by subject.

Subject bibliography

Of possibly greater utility than any of the above for specific
subject enquiries is:

> Statistics sources: a subject guide to data on
> industrial, business, social, educational, finan-
> cial, and other topics for the U.S. and selected
> foreign countries, edited by Paul Wasserman
> [and others], 4. ed. (Detroit, Gale, 1974).

Statistics

British library holdings

Unfortunately now somewhat out-of-date, but still useful is:

> Committee on Latin America: Latin American
> economic and social serials, [edited by K.I.
> Porter]. (London, Bingley, 1969, distributed
> by Latin America Books of York).

Items not recorded there may be sought through the
BRITISH UNION CATALOGUE OF LATIN AMERICANA
(q.v.), although it should be realised that the holdings of
several important libraries (e.g. the Official Publications
Library of the British Library Reference Division, the
Statistics and Market Intelligence Library, the University
of Sussex Institute of Development Studies Library and the
University of Warwick Library) are either not recorded
there, or recorded only in part. Material held at the British
Library of Political and Economic Science, London School of
Economics can be traced through A London bibliography of
the social sciences (see: PRINTED CATALOGUES). Material held in the Official Publications Library is available
as photocopies through the British Library Lending Division.

Censuses

Census returns are treated in the article 'CENSUSES' (q.v.).

Citation

Statistical publications present similar problems of citation
(and of tracing in catalogues) as other government publications; see the paragraph 'Citation' at the head of our section
on 'OFFICIAL PUBLICATIONS'.

[MR]

SUBJECT BIBLIOGRAPHY - GENERAL

Method

There are many ways to obtain, or compile, a subject bibliography, none of them completely satisfactorily. Your choice will depend on the nature of your subject, on how exhaustive a listing you need, how up-to-date you want it to be, and how many different types of material (books, articles, archives, official publications ...) you wish to include, but you will almost always have to combine several different approaches.

Your own library's subject catalogue is the simplest first step, and experience will soon teach you how far to rely on it: a good subject catalogue represents an enormous investment over the years in professional staff time. Your library may lack (or may have lacked in the past) the resources to achieve adequacy, and indeed you may still occasionally meet the attitude that only the author catalogue is really necessary: "if you are a scholar, sir, you will <u>know</u> which authors you wish to consult".

Many excellent library subject catalogues have, fortunately, been published; we indicate some of these in the section 'PRINTED CATALOGUES', but they may be hard to find. If you do any work in a North American library, you will probably meet the serried ranks of all the voluminous G.K. Hall catalogues the moment you enter their Latin American section. In this country, alas, even copies of the magnificent Texas Latin American collection catalogue can be counted on the fingers of one hand, and there was not a single copy of the Tulane University Latin American catalogue - probably unrivalled in its coverage of Middle America - until the British Library Reference Division recently decided to acquire one.

Your library's catalogue, or one of the printed catalogues, should have led you to one or more published bibliographies covering all or part of your subject. If not, you should find some via the bibliographies of bibliographies listed in our general section on 'BIBLIOGRAPHIES'. We also list a few

Method   (cont'd.)

of the more extensive subject bibliographies in the section
that follows: 'SUBJECT BIBLIOGRAPHY: MAJOR SUB-
JECTS'.

The foregoing may be supplemented, particularly if your
interests are geographically limited, by appropriate national bibliographies (see the section 'NATIONAL BIBLIO-
GRAPHY'), many of which permit a subject approach. Nor
should you overlook booksellers' catalogues, which are
often issued on a subject basis, or in a subject arrangement; they are also more up-to-date than most other
sources (see: 'BOOKSELLERS'). You are unlikely to find
these in your library's catalogue but should beg them from
its Latin American expert or the head of its book-ordering
or accessions department.

Most of the above are limited to monographs and other
books and pamphlets. Sources for locating periodical articles are discussed under 'PERIODICALS' (q.v.) but these
can never be quite up-to-date and if time permits, you
should browse through the last 18 months' or so issues of
leading periodicals in your field yourself.

Do not overlook other non-book materials that may be omit-
ted both from your library's catalogue and any bibliography
you find. Study in particular the sections in this guide on
DATA BANKS, NEWS & CURRENT AFFAIRS, MANU-
SCRIPTS & ARCHIVES, MICROFORM MATERIAL, and
THESES.

Finally, acquaint the Latin Americanist on your library staff
with your interests. He can be particularly helpful in draw-
ing your attention to material that is too new to have gotten
into the catalogue: libraries often have several weeks' or
even months' backlog of material waiting to be catalogued.

Subject bibliography - general

Arrangement

Subject catalogues and bibliographies can come in a variety of physical forms: cards in drawers, slips in sheaf binders, computer print-outs, microfiche and other forms of micro-photography, as well as printed books. There are, nevertheless, but two basic ways of arranging the material: alphabetic and classified. The criteria for selecting an appropriate alphabetical subject heading, and the variety of subject classification schemes are unfortunately legion, and a little preliminary study of its method of arrangement is essential whenever you use any subject reference tool for the first time. Be wary of over-reliance on posted notices about how to use a library catalogue; these have necessarily to be brief, and it is usually worthwhile asking the staff to explain the finer points.

[LH]

Introduction to the major disciplines

We have outlined the general principles of subject bibliography in the previous section, 'SUBJECT BIBLIOGRAPHY - GENERAL'. The following paragraphs make a few remarks about the main broad subject fields, suggesting (in most cases) an introductory text, an important bibliography and a specialist library or libraries.

Agriculture

A basic source is:

> Alvear Herrera, Gualberto Alfredo: Bibliografía de bibliografías agrícolas de América latina, 2.ed. (Turrialba, Costa Rica, Instituto interamericano de ciencias agrícolas, 1969) - the first edition was by Hugo Caceres Ramos, in 1967.

From the same Institute came:

> Caceres Ramos, Hugo: Guía de publicaciones periódicas agrícolas de America latina. (Turrialba, IIACA, 1966).

Too recent for inclusion in Alvear Herrera:

> Sable, Martin H.: Latin American agriculture; a bibliography on pioneer settlement, agricultural history and economics, rural sociology and population ... , agricultural cooperatives and credit. (Milwaukee, Center for Latin American studies of Wisconsin University, 1970).

There are also several relevant working papers in the Final report of the Fourteenth Seminar on the Acquisition of Latin American Library Materials, San Juan, PR, 1969 (Washington, O.A.S., 1970).

Agriculture (cont'd.)

Libraries interested in various aspects of agriculture in
Latin America (or the Commonwealth Caribbean) include
the Oxford Institute of Agricultural Economics library, the
library of the Royal Botanic Gardens at Kew, the Science
Reference Library, the library of the Tropical Products
Institute, and the library of Wye College of London University.

Anthropology

The standard handbooks on Amerindian life and culture are:

> Steward, Julian H., ed.: Handbook of South Ameri-
> can Indians, prepared in coöperation with the U.S.
> Department of State as a project of the Inter-
> departmental Committee on Cultural and Scien-
> tific Coöperation. (Washington, GPO, 7 vols,
> 1946-50) - Smithsonian Institution Bureau of
> American Ethnology Bulletin 143;

> Handbook of Middle American Indians; general
> editor, Robert Wauchope. (Austin, University
> of Texas Press, 1964-   ) - conceived on
> similar lines to the Steward Handbook, but on
> an even more ambitious scale; still in progress,
> vol 16 having come out in 1976.

Bibliographies include:

> Jasquith, James R.: "Bibliography of anthro-
> pological bibliographies of the Americas",
> América indígena 30(2), April 1970, pp.419-
> 469.

Subject bibliography - major subjects

Architecture

A fairly recent textbook covering all periods is:

> Castedo, Leopoldo: Historia del arte y de la arquitectura latinoamericana, 1.ed. 'corregida' (Santiago de Chile, Pomaire, 1970) - also available in translation from the first version: History of Latin American art and architecture from pre-Columbian times to the present. (London, Pall Mall, 1969).

The short bibliography in Castedo can be supplemented for the earlier period by:

> Gutiérrez, Ramón: Notas para una bibliografía hispanoamericana de arquitectura 1526-1875. (Resistencia, Universidad nacional del Nordeste, 1973).

The best library on the subject in the U.K. is the Sir Banister Fletcher Library of the Royal Institute of British Architects.

Art

There is a recent introductory text:

> Franco, Mrs. Jean: The modern culture of Latin America: society and the artist. Revised ed. (Harmondsworth, Penguin, 1970);

but the chief bibliography is now well out of date (and should be supplemented by the sections on 'Art' in the "Humanities" volumes of the Handbook of Latin American studies):

> Smith, Robert C., and Wilder, E.: A guide to the art of Latin America. (Washington, GPO, 1948).

The best library collection is probably that of the Victoria and Albert Museum.

Subject bibliography - major subjects

Economics

The literature of this subject is vast. A very first reading for the beginner might be:

> Benham, Frederic C., and Holley, H.A.: A short introduction to the economy of Latin America. (London, Oxford University Press, 1960).

A good bibliography, but one that will need supplementing for the last ten years is:

> Institut für Iberoamerika-Kunde, Hamburg: Wirtschaft und Entwicklung Lateinamerikas. (Hamburg, the Institute, 3 vols, 1967).

For economic history there is:

> Latin America: a guide to economic history 1830-1930, edited by Roberto Carlos Conde and Stanley J.Stein. (Berkeley, University of California Press, 1977).

Particularly relevant to economic studies is our section on 'STATISTICS'. See also 'NEWS & CURRENT AFFAIRS - OTHER SOURCES' for digests and surveys of economic development.

The outstanding library in the field is the British Library of Political and Economic Science at the London School of Economics. Also important is the Economics Department Library of Lloyds Bank International in Pall Mall (which derives in part from the library of the former Bank of London and South America). Among the many university collections with good coverage of Latin American economics we might mention the Oxford Institute of Economics and Statistics Library and the library of the University of Sussex Institute of Development Studies.

Subject bibliography - major subjects

Education

Routledge & Kegan Paul's "World education series"
includes:

> Gale, Laurence: Education and development in
> Latin America ... (London, Routledge; New
> York, Praeger, 1969).

A library catalogue serving as an up-to-date bibliography is:

> Partin, Emmett M.: Resource guide to materials on
> education in Latin America currently available in
> the M.H. Penniman Memorial Library of Education.
> (Philadelphia, Penniman Library of the University
> of Pennsylvania, 1974).

In the field of tertiary education there is a succession of bibliographies by Philip G. Altbach (the second in collaboration with David H. Kelly): Higher education in developing countries: a select bibliography [1945-1968] (Cambridge, Mass., Harvard Center for International Affairs, 1970), Higher education in developing nations 1969-1974 (New York, Praeger, 1975) and Comparative higher education abroad (New York, Praeger, 1976).

Latin American education is not a subject well covered in British libraries. The best collection is probably that of the Comparative Education Library of the London Institute of Education.

Geography

The standard work is:

> James, Preston E.: Latin America, 4.ed. (New
> York, Odyssey, 1969).

Geography (cont'd.)

A good bibliographical guide is lacking; you will have either
to use a general geographical bibliography, such as the
Bibliographie géographique internationale, or hunt out something more specific (e.g. limited to one particular country).
See also our section 'MAPS & ATLASES'.

The largest library collection is that of the Royal Geographical Society. Important within their regions of interest
are the libraries of the Royal Commonwealth Society and the
Scott Polar Research Institute of Cambridge University. We
may also mention the libraries of University College, London, and of the School of Geography, Oxford.

Government and politics

For an introduction:

> Needler, Martin C., ed.: Political systems of
> Latin America, 2.ed.   (New York, Van Nostrand
> Reinhold, 1970).

Bibliographies include:

> Blanksten, George I.: "Bibliography on Latin
> American politics and government", Inter-
> American review of bibliography, 4(3), Jly/
> Sep. 1954, pp.191-124;

> Chilcote, Ronald H.: Revolution and structural
> change in Latin America: a bibliography on
> ideology, development and the radical left 1930-
> 1965.   (Stanford, Hoover Institution on War,
> Revolution and Peace, 2 vols, 1970);

> Schaeffer, Jürgen: Bibliographie zur Politik und
> Zeitgeschichte der iberamerikanischen Länder.
> (Hamburg, Institut für Iberoamerika-Kunde, 1965).

Subject bibliography - major subjects

Government and politics (cont'd.)

See also the sections 'LAW AND LEGISLATION', 'NEWS & CURRENT AFFAIRS' and 'OFFICIAL PUBLICATIONS'.

Relevant libraries include those of the Royal Institute of International Affairs, of Saint Antony's College, Oxford and of the London School of Economics and Political Science.

History

A recent general history is:

> Collier, Simon D.W.: From Cortés to Castro, an introduction to the history of Latin America 1492-1973. (London, Secker and Warburg, 1974).

The chief general bibliographies are:

> Griffin, Charles C.: Latin America, a guide to the historical literature. (Austin, University of Texas Press, 1971);

> Humphreys, Robert [alias Robin] Arthur: Latin American history, a guide to the literature in English. (London, Oxford University Press, 1958) - still valuable, despite its date and the exclusion of Spanish and other foreign-language material;

> Sánchez, Alonso B.: Fuentes de la historia española e hispanoamericana, 3.ed. (Madrid, 3 vols & 'suplemento', 1952).

Early (i. e. pre-1800) historians are well covered in:

> Wilgus, Alvar Curtis: The historiography of Latin America: a guide to historical writing 1500-1800. (Metuchen, Scarecrow, 1975).

For guides to source material, see our section on 'MANU-SCRIPTS AND ARCHIVES'.

History   (cont'd.)

Professor Humphreys was largely responsible for the fine
library collections on Latin American history at University
College, London, and at the London Institute of Historical
Research. Many other libraries have good Latin American
history collections, among them the Bodleian, Cambridge
University Library, the British Library Reference Division,
Liverpool University Library (especially for Brazil and
Peru) and Essex University Library (especially for Chile,
Brazil and Uruguay).

Linguistics

> Primus, Mrs. Wilma J.: Creole and pidgin lan-
> guages in the Caribbean: an annotated biblio-
> graphy.   (London, Library Association, unpub-
> lished Fellowship thesis, 1974) - presumably an
> enlargement of her Creole and pidgin languages
> in the Caribbean: a select bibliography.   (St.
> Augustine, Trinidad, Library of the University of
> the West Indies, 1972);

> Reinecke, John E., and others: A bibliography of
> pidgin and creole languages.   (Honolulu, Univer-
> sity Press of Hawaii, 1975);

> Tovar, Antonio: Catálogo de las lenguas de América
> del sur: enumeración ... con bibliografía ...
> (Buenos Aires, Sudamericana, 1961).

For Spanish and Portuguese in the Americas there is:

> Rohlfs, Gerhard: Manual de filología hispánica:
> guía bibliográfica, crítica y metódica.   (Bogotá,
> Instituto Caro y Cuervo, 1957).

The above may be supplemented by such works as the Year's
work in modern language studies (Cambridge, 1932-   ) and
Romanische Bibliographie   (Tübingen, annually, 1965-   ).

Linguistics   (cont'd.)

Material on Amerindian linguistics has been collected by the libraries of the University of Saint Andrews and the University of London School of Oriental and African Studies.

Material on Spanish and Portuguese will be found in the libraries of practically every university with a commitment to Latin American Studies. In the cases of the universities of Cambridge, Oxford and London, the principal collections will be found in the Modern and Medieval Languages Libraries, the Taylorian and King's College Library, respectively.

Literature of Brazil

One of the very few introductions specially written for the English-speaking reader (now unfortunately rather outdated) is:

> Putnam, Samuel: Marvelous journey, a survey of four centuries of Brazilian writing.   (New York, Knopf, 1948, reprinted Octagon, 1971).

Combining a "Síntese crítico-histórica" (by Brito Broca) with a "Bibliografia" (by José Galante de Sousa) is:

> Broca, José Brito: Introdução ao estudo da literatura brasileira.   (Rio de Janeiro, Instituto nacional do livro, 1963) - attribution of authorship by the National Union Catalog to Brito Broca, despite the substantially larger contribution by Galante de Sousa, and the absence of both names from the title page is alas typical of the vagaries of library cataloguing!

Other bibliographies are given in the paragraph 'Literary bio-bibliography: Brazilian authors' in our section on AUTHOR & PERSONAL BIBLIOGRAPHY (q.v.).

Literature of Brazil (cont'd.)

University libraries with sizeable collections of Brazilian literature include those of Essex, Glasgow and Liverpool. In London the largest university collection is that of King's College.

Literature of Hispanic America

A good recent text is:

> Franco, Mrs. Jean: An introduction to Spanish American literature. (Cambridge, Cambridge University Press, 1971).

Recent bibliographies include:

> Bryant, Shasta M.: A selective bibliography of bibliographies of Hispanic American literature, 2.ed., greatly expanded and revised. (Austin, University of Texas Press, 1976);

> Rela, Walter: Guía bibliográfica de la literatura hispanoamericana desde el siglo diez y nueve hasta 1970. (Buenos Aires, Casa Pardo, 1971).

See also the paragraph 'Literary bio-bibliography: Spanish American authors' in our section on AUTHOR & PERSONAL BIBLIOGRAPHY.

So many libraries have substantial collections of Spanish American literature that it is only worth our while pointing out places with special strengths in some of the less usually favoured literatures: Colombian literature at the Taylorian (Oxford), Chilean literature at the Universities of Essex and Glasgow, Peruvian literature at Liverpool University, Bolivian and Uruguayan literatures at the University of Essex.

Subject bibliography - major subjects

Literature of the West Indies

A general survey of the English-speaking Caribbean which contains a good bibliography of Jamaican literature is:

Alleyne, Alvona: "Literary publishing in the English-speaking Caribbean", Twenty-first Seminar on the Acquisition of Latin American Library Materials, Bloomington (Ind.), 1976, (Working paper B-9).

Other sources are:

Keane, Mrs. Christiane: Commonwealth literature 1945-1975: a guide to the sources. (London, Library Association, unpublished Fellowship thesis, 1976);

McDowell, Robert E.: Bibliography of literature from Guyana. (Arlington, Texas, Sable Publishing, 1975);

New, William H.: Critical writings on Commonwealth literatures: a selective bibliography to 1970, with a list of theses and dissertations. (University Park, Pennsylvania State University Press, 1975) - "West Indies" pp.270-281 & 311-312.

A useful library catalogue is:

Watson, Karl S.: Literature of the English- and French-speaking West Indies in the University of Florida libraries: a bibliography. (Gainesville, University of Florida Libraries, 1971).

See also the paragraph 'Literary bio-bibliography: West-Indian authors' in our section on AUTHOR & PERSONAL BIBLIOGRAPHY.

Literature of the West Indies (cont'd.)

There are collections of West Indian literature at the Royal
Commonwealth Society Library, the Commonwealth Institute
Library and at the libraries of the universities of Manchester, Leeds, Kent and Aberdeen (amongst others). For details consult:

> Commonwealth Institute, London. Working party
> on library holdings of Commonwealth literature.
> A handbook of library holdings of Commonwealth
> literature in the United Kingdom, compiled and
> edited by Gail Wilson.   (London, The Working
> Party, 1971).

Medicine

Although there are hardly any general guides to the whole
region, the literature of some individual countries is quite
well documented. In the case of Brazil, for instance, there
is the current Bibliografia brasileira de medicina (begun in
1939, but with predecessors covering right back to 1860), and
many specialised bibliographies. See: 'NATIONAL BIBLIO-
GRAPHY', and also:

> St. Denis, Gaston P.: "Sources of information in
> the bio-medical sciences in Latin America",
> Fourteenth Seminar on the Acquisition of Latin
> American Library Materials, San Juan, PR, 1969,
> (Working paper 18: pp.133-143 of vol 2 of the
> Final report ...)

Current material is collected by the library of the London
School of Hygiene and Tropical Medicine (whose dictionary
catalogue was published by G.K. Hall of Boston, Mass.in 1967,
with a supplement in 1971). Historical material is collected
by the Historical Medical Library of the Wellcome Institute
of the History of Medicine, which has a special Latin American library.

Subject bibliography - major subjects

Science and technology

The standard international tools will cover anything written on or from the region which is of more than local interest - that is (mainly) subjects in which geography or climate has intrinsic relevance, such as geology, botany, zoology, or meteorology. These subjects are usually also well covered in general bibliographies of Latin America (see: 'BIBLIO-GRAPHIES - GENERAL').

Otherwise it is necessary to consult sources dealing with the scientific and technical output of individual countries. In the case of Brazil, for instance, the Instituto brasileiro de bibliografia e documentação produces regular (usually annual) bibliographies of books and articles in the fields of chemistry, engineering, mathematics, physics, technology and zoology, and an annual Pesquisas em processo no Brasil, whilst the Departamento nacional da produção mineral has been producing for many years now regular guides to material on geology and mining.

The Final report and working papers of the Fourteenth Seminar on the Acquisition of Latin American Library Materials, San Juan de Puerto Rico, 1969 (Washington, OAS, 1970) contains a number of contributions on the bibliography of science and technology.

The best general library for Latin American science and technology is the British Library's Science Reference Library. The Bayswater branch concentrates on the life sciences, whilst technology (including patents and trade mark journals) is at Holborn (the old Patent Office Library). You will however find certain individual subjects better covered by various special libraries: the collection at the Royal Botanic Gardens (Kew) library, for instance, is unrivalled in the fields of plant taxonomy, floras, and plant anatomy, cytology, genetics and physiology, and is an excellent resource also for horticulture, forestry, tropical agriculture, economic botany and botanical exploration.

Science and technology   (cont'd.)

We might also mention here:

> Hilton, Ronald: The scientific institutions of
> Latin America, with special reference to their
> organization and information facilities.   (Stan-
> ford, California Institute of International Studies,
> 1970).

Social sciences

The social sciences embrace so many subjects that it is difficult to suggest an introductory text covering the whole
field. Perhaps:

> Heath, Dwight B., and Adams, R.N.: Contem-
> porary cultures and societies of Latin America
> and the Caribbean.   (New York, Random House,
> 1965).

Similarly, most bibliographies limit themselves to particular
branches of the social sciences. Fairly general and not too
out-of-date is:

> Klein, Maria Teresa: Bibliographie zur Sociologie
> und Demographie Lateinamerikas.   (Hamburg,
> Institut für Iberoamerika-Kunde, 1968).

The prime U.K. library with coverage of all the social
sciences is that of the London School of Economics, but most
good general Latin American collections will be found useful,
whilst various specialised libraries are important within
their fields of interest (e.g. Latin American law at the London Institute of Advanced Legal Studies).

[LH, PN]

THESES

Significance and availability

Much important material is contained in unpublished theses
and dissertations, yet relatively little use is made of them
by researchers. We hope the following notes will help make
them more accessible.

Although the words 'thesis' and 'dissertation' are often
used interchangeably, it may be assumed that, in American
usage, a 'dissertation' will always be doctoral work, whilst
a 'thesis' will usually be at mastership level.

As will become apparent, most sources of information on
theses limit themselves to those accepted for doctorates.
Where mastership theses are included, this is usually done
for the M.Phil (or equivalent) only: theses produced as a
part requirement for a taught M.A. are very seldom listed.
Often the only way to learn about these (or to consult them)
is by a direct approach to the individual academic department or faculty of the university concerned.

Regulations for the loan and use of U.K. theses differ from
institution to institution, but the British Library Lending
Division attempts to collect in original or on microfilm all
doctoral theses currently produced in this country. Major
centres of Latin American activity so covered include the
universities of Cambridge (from 1968), Glasgow (from 1975),
London (from 1974) and Oxford (from 1972). Not yet participating (January 1978) are Essex and Liverpool. For further
details, enquire of the Inter-Library Lending section of your
library. Library Association Fellowship theses (some of
which feature in this Guide) can also be got through normal
inter-library lending procedures.

The British Library Lending Division can also supply copies
of North American theses listed in Dissertation abstracts
international (see paragraph on U.S. theses, below), from
1970, and sometimes earlier. Continental European theses
(which the BLLD acquires only in response to specific

requests) can be found, from last century onwards, in the
Bodleian (which has an extensive dissertation card index),
the British Library Reference Division, and elsewhere.
Consult:

> Johnson, Roger S.: Foreign theses in British
> libraries. (Cardiff, SCONUL, 1971).

International guides

The most general work is:

> Reynolds, Michael M.: A guide to theses and dis-
> sertations: an annotated international bibliography
> of bibliographies. (Detroit, Gale, 1975) - particu-
> larly useful for information on theses from
> countries not discussed below.

There is also:

> Davinson, Donald E.: Theses and dissertations
> and information sources. (London, Bingley,
> 1970).

Specifically on Latin American subjects is:

> Brown, Larry C.: "Report on lists of doctoral
> dissertations and masters' theses on Latin
> America", Latin American research review,
> 6(3), Fall 1971, pp.127-129.

International listings of theses on special areas or subjects
within Latin America include:

> Baa, Enid M.: Theses on Caribbean topics, 1778-
> 1968. (St. Thomas, Bureau of Public Libraries &
> Museums, 1968; reprinted, San Juan, University of
> Puerto Rico Press, 1970) - two separate author
> listings of 1005 dissertations and 236 theses:

primarily work done in North America, the U.K., and France. Updated by the annual "List of doctoral research on the Caribbean and circum-Caribbean accepted by American, British and Canadian universities" in each second quarterly issue of Caribbean studies;

Hanson, Carl A.: Dissertations on Iberian and Latin American history: an interdisciplinary bibliography of dissertations completed in the U.S., Great Britain, Canada and Ireland, 1889-1969. (Troy, Whitston, 1975) - 3564 titles, arranged chronologically and by subject;

Hanson, Carl A.: "Dissertations on Luso-Brazilian topics: a bibliography of dissertations completed in the United States, Great Britain and Canada, 1892-1970", Americas, 30, 1973-1974, pp.251-267 & 373-403;

New, William H.: Critical writings on Commonwealth literatures: a selective bibliography to 1970, with a list of theses and dissertations. (University Park, Pennsylvania State University Press, 1975) - theses on West Indian literature, pp.311-312;

Zubatsky, David S.: "An international guide to lists of theses and dissertations in the Hispanic languages and literatures", Hispania, 55(2), May 1972, pp.293-302.

Theses

Guides to British theses

Current material is listed annually in:

> Theses in Latin American studies at British universities, in progress and recently completed, 1966/67- (London, Institute of Latin American Studies, 1967-) - attempts to be comprehensive of doctoral theses; inclusion of mastership theses at discretion of reporting institution. Author & subject indexes.

Retrospective listing is provided by:

> Hodcroft, F.W.: "Theses in Hispanic subjects approved for higher degrees by British and Irish universities 1972-1974, with some additional earlier titles", Bulletin of Hispanic studies, 52(4), Oct. 1975, pp.325-344 - supplements and corrects some errors in:

> Jones, Cyril A.: "Theses in Hispanic subjects approved for higher degrees by British universities to 1971", Bulletin of Hispanic studies, 49(4), Oct. 1972, pp.325-354;

> Zubatsky, David S.: Doctoral dissertations in history and the social sciences on Latin America and the Caribbean, accepted by universities in the United Kingdom 1920-72. (London, Institute of Latin American Studies, 1973),

- and by the comprehensive:

> Bilboul, Roger R., and Kent, F.L.: Retrospective index to theses of Great Britain and Ireland 1716-1950. (Oxford, European Bibliographical Centre/ Clio Press, 5 vols, 1976-77) - vol 1 relates to the social sciences and the humanities, vols 2-5 to the sciences; author and subject indexes.

Theses

Guides to United States theses

There are two annual lists of North American theses on
Latin American topics, appearing in periodicals. A "Pro-
visional list of dissertations on Latin American topics" by
Jane Garner has been published in the September issue of
the Latin American Studies Association newsletter since
1973. Hispania issues a list of "Dissertations in the Hispanic languages and literatures", usually in its May issue;
this began appearing in 1935, but covers from 1915 (although mastership theses have been excluded since 1949).
There is also a "Research in progress" section of the
Luso-Brazilian review which has appeared spasmodically
in some winter numbers; this arranges doctoral theses and
post-doctoral research under broad geographical areas,
subdivided by discipline.

Current work may also be traced through Xerox University
Microfilm's Dissertation abstracts (mentioned above),
which appears monthly in two sections: A. "The Humanities"
and B. "The Sciences and engineering"; abstracts of theses
are given, arranged by subject (e.g. "History: Latin America"), with keyword-in-title and author indexes. In 1976 this
became Dissertation abstracts international, and added a
third section, C. "European abstracts". As yet participation
in the new section is limited (only two U.K. institutions
contribute), and it is only a quarterly. Even North American participation (sections A. & B.) is still not total, and
many institutions have only begun to contribute quite recently (e.g. the University of Chicago from 1974). Copies
of theses listed may be purchased, in either Xerox or
microfilm, and there is a relevant sectional catalogue:

> Latin America: a catalog of dissertations. (Ann
> Arbor, Xerox University Microfilms, 1974).

A complete listing of all doctoral dissertations accepted by
American and Canadian universities is claimed by the same
publisher's American doctoral dissertations, issued annually on an academic year basis and arranged by institutions

Guides to United States theses   (cont'd.)

under disciplines - e.g. 'Economics, agricultural', 'History, modern', 'Language & literature, modern', making a search for Latin American topics tedious in the extreme. There is an author, but no subject, index.

The principal retrospective index to North American theses is:

> Comprehensive dissertation index 1861-1972.
> (Ann Arbor, Xerox University Microfilms,
> 37 vols, 1974).

Among a variety of retrospective listings of Latin American theses that restrict themselves to particular disciplines, countries, institutions or periods, we may mention:

> Chaffee, Wilber A., and Griffin, H.M.: Disser-
> tations on Latin America by U.S. historians
> 1960-1970: a bibliography.   (Austin, Institute
> of Latin American Studies, 1973) - about 450
> theses, arranged by country;

> Chatham, James R., and Ruiz-Fornells, E.:
> Dissertations in Hispanic languages and litera-
> tures: an index of dissertations completed in
> the United States and Canada 1876-1966.   (Lex-
> ington, University Press of Kentucky, 1970) - a
> classified list covering comparative literature
> and applied linguistics, including those of the
> Peninsula;

> Griffin, Ernst C., and Minkel, C.W.: A biblio-
> graphy of theses and dissertations on Latin
> America by U.S. geographers, 1960-1970.
> (Washington, Pan American Institute of Geo-
> graphy and History, 1970) - arranged by country,
> and supplementary to:

Theses

Guides to United States theses   (cont'd.)

Browning, Clyde E.: Bibliography of dissertations in geography 1901-1969.   (Chapel Hill, Department of geography of the University of North Carolina, 1970) - index by regions;

Kantor, Harry: A bibliography of unpublished doctoral dissertations and masters' theses dealing with the governments, politics and international relations of Latin America. (Gainesville, Inter-American bibliographical and library association, 1953);

Kidder, Frederick E.: "Doctoral dissertations in Latin American area studies, 1959-63", Americas, 18(3), Jan. 1962, pp.304-310; 19(2), Oct. 1962, pp.191-197; 20(2), Oct. 1963, pp.208-214; 21(2), Oct. 1964, pp.196-205;

Ramos, Dulce Helena Alvares Pessoa: "Levantamento das pesquisas sobre assuntos brasileiros feitas em universidades americanas 1960-1970", Revista de história (São Paulo), 49(99), 1974, pp.281-308;

University of Texas at Austin. Institute of Latin American Studies: Latin American research and publications at the University of Texas at Austin 1893-1969.   (Austin, 1971);

Zubatsky, David S.: "U.S. doctoral dissertations on Cuban studies in the twentieth century", Cuban studies newsletter, 4(2), Jun. 1974, pp.35-55.

Guides to Canadian theses

Most of the guides in the last paragraph include Canadian theses. There is also a separate list of theses currently accepted by Canadian universities:

Theses

Guides to Canadian theses   (cont'd.)

Canadian theses / Thèses canadiennes, 1960/61-
(Ottawa, National Library of Canada, 1962-   ) -
arranged by subject, subdivided by university,

and a retrospective list of Canadian theses on the Caribbean
from 1927 to 1970:

Hills, Theo L.: Caribbean topics: theses in Canadian university libraries, 3.ed.   (Montreal, Centre
for developing-area studies of McGill University,
1971) - arranged by institution and sub-divided by
main subject area (as history, geography, sociology,
economics).

French theses

French doctoral theses are reported currently in:

France. Direction des bibliothèques de France:
Catalogue des thèses de doctorat soutenues
devant les universités françaises.   Nouvelle
série, 1959-   (Paris, Cercle de la Librairie,
1960-   ) - arranged by faculty, subdivided by
university and type of doctorate. Author index.

Giving a retrospective listing from 1954 to 1974 is:

"Catalogue des thèses et mémoires sur l'Amérique latine soutenues en France", Cahiers des
Amériques latines, 4, 1969, pp.145-194 (covering
to 1969) & 9/10, 1974, pp.282-366 (covering 1970-
74) - arranged by country, subdivided by subject.

For earlier years there is also:

France. Direction des bibliothèques de France:
Catalogue des thèses de doctorat soutenues
devant les universités françaises 1884/5-1958.
(Paris, 1885-1959).

Theses

Low Countries

The Centrum voor studie en documentatie van Latijns Amerika of Amsterdam University ('CEDLA') includes a "Registro de los estudios belgas y neerlandeses sobre América latina" (articles, conference papers and monographs as well as theses, both in progress and recently completed) in its semi-annual Boletín de estudios latinoamericanos y del Caribe.

Other countries

There are numerous other listings of national theses. These can be traced through the Reynolds bibliography given first in the paragraph "International guides" above. General European sources are also included (despite the title) in P.G. Short's article "British theses" in the SCONUL Information Services Group's ISG news, 5, Apr. 1977, pp.21-23.

Library Association fellowship theses

Theses accepted for the Fellowship of the Library Association with Latin American relevance (on the bibliography and libraries of the region) are listed to March 1977 on page 4 of:

> Hallewell, Laurence: "Latin American activities in the United Kingdom", Twenty-second Seminar on the Acquisition of Latin American Library Materials, Gainesville FL, 1977, (working paper A-6).

Post-doctoral work

A few of the above titles include post-doctoral and other research, but this is discussed further in our section 'UNIVERSITY STUDY & RESEARCH'.

[CRS]

TRANSLATION

Directories of translators

> Flegon, A.: Who's who in translation and inter-
> preting. (London, Flegon Press, 1967);

> Millard, Patricia: Directory of technical and
> scientific translators and services. (London,
> Crosby Lockwood, 1968) - lists translators and
> translation bureaux alphabetically, with indexes
> of languages and of subjects specialities sub-
> arranged by language.

More up-to-date information is available from the Translators' Guild of the Institute of Linguistics, who regularly
publish a list of their members with their specializations.
Advertisements by translators will be found in the monthly
Aslib information (London, Aslib, January 1973-   ).

British Library translation service

The British Library Lending Division provides an ad hoc
translation service for periodical articles, at a current rate
of £1 per typed A4 page from Spanish and Portuguese: other
languages range from 75p. per page (from French) to £1.40
per page (from Japanese). Apply through the Inter-Library
Lending Department of your library.

The BLLD also sponsors translations of books, mainly in
scientific and technical fields; see its Translated books
available from BLLD (1976).

Dictionaries

See the section 'LANGUAGE DICTIONARIES'.

Literary translations

A short bibliography of bibliographies of English translations
of Latin American literary works is given at the end of our
section 'BIBLIOGRAPHIES - MATERIAL IN ENGLISH'.
[LH]

UNIVERSITY STUDY & RESEARCH

Latin American studies in higher education institutions of the U.K.

Although significant British academic interest in Latin America began at least as long ago as the 1920's, the framework in which present day researchers work is largely the result of the 1965 report of the Committee on Latin America of the University Grants Committee under the chairmanship of Dr.J.H. Parry.

The report led to the creation of five "Parry centres" of Latin American studies, at the Universities of Cambridge, Glasgow, Liverpool, London and Oxford, at the same time as the then newly founded University of Essex was building up what was virtually a sixth centre of study on the region. The report also provided some stimulus for Latin American studies elsewhere. Even discounting this, the area has formed a natural focus of interest for economists, political scientists, anthropologists, Hispanists etc. Thus, despite a concentration of work at the six universities named, there is much activity elsewhere, some of it outstanding in particular fields (e.g. Amerindian linguistics at St.Andrews).

At least two of the newly emergent polytechnics (Portsmouth and Wolverhampton) and one other non-university institution (Ealing College of Further Education in West London) have given a special place to Latin American studies as undergraduate degree courses (in constrast to universities which, for the most part, offer Latin American courses at the postgraduate level, or as special subjects or options in first degree courses centred on a traditional discipline).

Information on courses

The syllabuses of relevant U.K. university courses are outlined in the annual:

> Latin American studies in the universities of the United Kingdom, 1, 1966/67- (London, University of London Institute of Latin American Studies, 1967-   ).

Information on courses   (cont'd.)

As this omits non-university courses, it should be supplemented by a more general guide, such as Which university (London, Haymarket, annual): despite its title this does include polytechnics and colleges.

Surveys of courses, research projects etc. at United Kingdom institutions also appear from time to time in the Bulletin of the Society for Latin American Studies.

Research in progress

The London Institute of Latin American Studies publishes an annual

> Staff research in progress or recently completed in the humanities and the social sciences, 1, 1968/69-   (London, University of London Institute of Latin American Studies, 1969-   ) - a supplement to its Latin American studies, under which title you may find it indexed in some library catalogues.

There are several other sources of information on current research. The most important is probably the "Current research inventory" of North-American post-doctoral research which appears regularly in the Latin American research review (Austin, University of Texas Press, 1965-   ). For work on Brazil there is the somewhat irregular "Research in progress" section of the Luso-Brazilian review (Madison, University of Wisconsin, 1964-   ). European research is reported in the Boletín informativo sobre estudios latinoamericanos (Amsterdam, Centrum voor Studie en Dokumentatie van Latijns Amerika, 1965-   ).

For research by students, see the section 'THESES'.

University study & research

Research institutes - United Kingdom

Latin American centres in the U.K. include the following.
While some are active centres of research, others merely
centralise information about research on the region carried
out elsewhere in their universities:

Cambridge (Centre of Latin American Studies,
    History Faculty Building, West Road,
    Cambridge CB3 9DR);

Colchester (Latin American Centre, University
    of Essex, Wivenhoe Park, Colchester ,
    Essex, CO4 3SQ);

Glasgow (Institute of Latin American Studies,
    5 University Gardens, Glasgow, Scotland
    G12 8QT);

Liverpool (Centre for Latin-American Studies,
    86/88 Bedford Street South, Liverpool);

London (Institute of Latin American Studies,
    31 Tavistock Square, London WC1H 9HA);

Oxford (Latin American Centre, Saint Antony's
    College, 21 Winchester Road, Oxford OX2 6NA).

Note that the Latin America Centre at 17 Hoxton Square,
London N1 is not a research institute but a social centre 'for
Latin Americans and British people interested in Latin
America'.

Research institutes abroad

A directory of "Latin American research centers" in North
America occupies pages 73 to 106 of:

Haro, Robert P.: Latin American research in the
United States and Canada: a guide and directory.
(Chicago, American Library Association, 1971).

223

Research institutes abroad   (cont'd.)

Addresses of research institutes in Europe (East and West) are given on pages 20-21 and 28 of:

> Latinamerika-Institutet i Stockholm: Handledning vid samhällsvetenskaplig och historisk forskning rörande Latinamerika, utgiven för Nordiska samfundet för Latinamerika-forskning, 2. ed.   (Stockholm, the Institute, 1974);

and there is more detailed information on "Centros de estudios sobre América latina en Europa" on pages 36-49 of:

> Mörner, Magnus, and Campa, R.: Investigación en ciencias sociales e históricas sobre América latina: enfoque preliminar para una guía.   (Rome, CEISAL, 1975).

For institutes in Latin America itself, see our section 'DIRECTORIES'.

Information on British academics

The "List of teachers" in the annual Latin American studies in the universities of the United Kingdom (above) gives, under each university, both staff directly engaged in teaching Latin American courses and those with Latin American interests not so engaged. Information is limited to surname and initials, degrees, position now held and current principal research interests. Rather fuller details can be found (for those Britons included in it) in our next item:

European Latin-Americanists

Full names, birth year, home address, present appointment and date, and publications, are among the information in:

European Latin-Americanists   (cont'd.)

Latinoamericanistas europeos [edited by] Adriaan van Oss. (Amsterdam, Centrum voor studie en dokumentatie van Latijns Amerika, 1974) - revision of the 1969 Directorio de latinoamericanistas europeos, edited by Harry Hoetink and others.

Canadian Latin-Americanists

Tatlow, Frederick J.: Directory of scholars in Latin American teaching and research in Canada, 1969-70, 2.ed.   (Ottawa, Association of universities and colleges of Canada, 1970?).

United States Latin-Americanists

Similar details to the Van Oss directory, plus an indication of linguistic proficiencies, are given for 'personnel with specialised knowledge of Latin America' in the U.S.A. in:

United States of America. Library of Congress. Hispanic Foundation: National directory of Latin Americanists ...: biographies of 2,695 specialists in the social sciences and humanities. (Washington, GPO, 1971).

Scholars from Latin America

Historians are listed in:

Pan American Institute of Geography and History. Commission on history: Guía de personas que cultivan la historia de América, [2.ed.] al cuidado de Juan Domingo Vidargas del Moral. (Mexico City, the Institute, 1967) - which may be supplemented by:

Scholars from Latin America   (cont'd.)

> Morales Padrón, Francisco: "Guía de profesores
> de historia de América en universidades ibero-
> americanas", Historia y bibliografía american-
> istas, 17, 1971, pp.45-79.

For sociologists there is:

> Remmling, Gunter W.: South American sociolo-
> gists, a directory.   (Austin, University of
> Texas, 1966).

Caribbean scholars

The background, experience, publications and address of
scholars in the fields of archaeology, geography, history,
social sciences, folklore, law and linguistics relating to the
Antilles and coastal Central America are detailed in:

> Universidad de Puerto Rico. Institute of
> Caribbean Science [afterwards 'of Caribbean
> studies']: Directory of Caribbean scholars,
> 2.ed., by W.A. Trembley.   (Rio Piedras, the
> Institute, 1964).

[BN]

A D D E N D A

Societies & associations - continental Europe, p.184

    Add: Société des Américanistes
           Musée de l'homme, Place du Trocadéro, 75116 Paris

Subject bibliography - literature of West Indies, p.208

The Gail Wilson bibliography has now been revised and
enlarged as:

        Handbook of library holdings of Commonwealth
        literature: United Kingdom and Europe. (Boston Spa,
        British Library Lending Division, 1977).

Translation - directories of translators, p.220

Since 1975 the Guild of Professional Translators of
Philadelphia has been issuing an annual Translator
referral directory covering translators in 16 countries
competent in a total of 46 languages.